EDINBURGH
Lore and Legend

George Street, St Andrew's Church and Lord Melville's Monument
(overleaf)

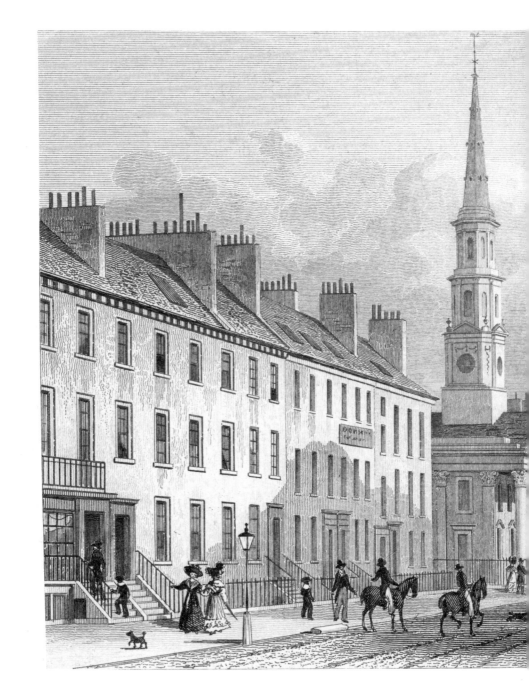

EDINBURGH

Lore and Legend

MARION LOCHHEAD

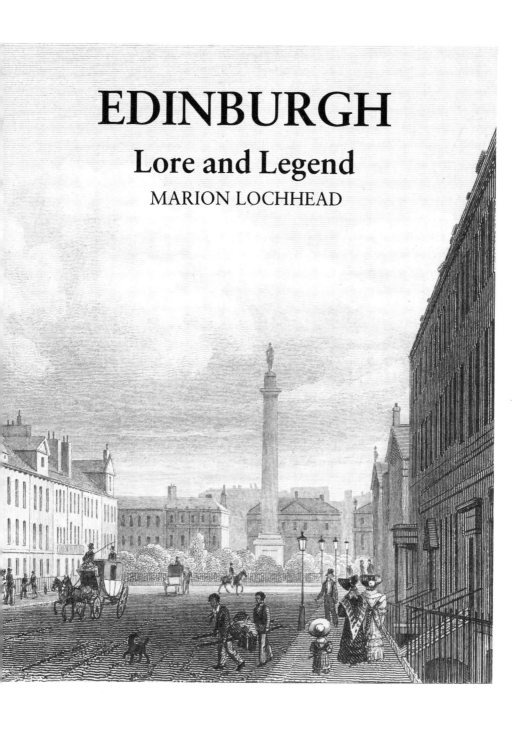

Robert Hale Limited
Clerkenwell House
Clerkenwell Green
London EC1R 0HT

British Library Cataloguing Publication Data

Lochhead, Marion
Edinburgh: lore and legend.
1. Tales – Scotland – Edinburgh (Lothian)
2. Legends – Scotland – Edinburgh (Lothian)
3. Edinburgh (Lothian) – Fiction
I. Title
398.2'32 4134   GR145.E3

ISBN 0-7090-2815-6

Set in Sabon by Rowland Phototypesetting Limited
Printed in Great Britain by
St Edmundsbury Press Limited, Bury St Edmunds, Suffolk
and bound in Edinburgh by
Hunter & Foulis Limited

Contents

By the same author

Portrait of the Scott Country
Magic and Witchcraft of the Borders

Illustrations

All engravings are taken from *Modern Athens or Edinburgh in the nineteenth century* by Thomas H. Shepherd (1829) with the exception of the following: *Kay's Original Portraits* by John Kay; 37: *The Trial of Katharine Nairn* by William Roughead

Introduction

Edinburgh, that 'ancient and famous metropolis of the north', as Stevenson called it, is one of the most complex of cities, almost as complex and as fascinating as Rome: a capital city and a collection of villages, of *quartiers*, like Paris, each with its own character. It is a city of culture and crime, of solid history, of tradition and legend, near enough the Borders to share the heritage of ballads and of magic.

'So you are living in the university *quartier*,' a friend said, when I went to live in Edinburgh in a high flat overlooking the Meadows, within easy distance of the university and of its library, very near George Square and the home of our most illustrious villager in that region, Walter Scott.

The complexity comes from centuries of history, factual and legendary, the one as convincing and valuable as the other. Its citizens over the centuries have ranged in morals from the douce,* respectable kirk-going and the exalted intellectual to the rowdy and the downright wicked, the latter sometimes with more than a touch of sheer black devilish evil in them. It is a city of the law and of the lawless, of the godly (who do not appear very often in these tales), the mischievous and the downright bad.

Edinburgh is the true home of Jekyll and Hyde, although Stevenson set that drama in London. Part of the inspiration comes from the true history of Deacon Brodie, that versatile and adroit master of two trades: the respectable one of cabinet-making and the other of housebreaking and burglary. Mr Hyde goes beyond the Deacon in wickedness, however; the Deacon is lawless rather than evil. Hyde's closest kinsman is Major Weir (p. 93), known to his devotees as Angelical Thomas.

A city of the Kirk, especially in May when the fathers and brethren assemble in debate and in decorous jocundity, the Moderator wearing his eighteenth-century costume of knee-

---

* All asterisks refer to the Glossary, p. 187

Edinburgh from Craigleith

breeches, ruffles, cocked hat; a city perhaps even more, and essentially of the law: Parliament House at the centre; a city in itself of traditions and customs, rank and formality, writers, advocates and senators. Scott's father was a writer, or solicitor, he himself an advocate, clerk to the court, Sheriff of Selkirk forbye,* as well as a novelist of world fame. There is no getting away from Scott; he will recur in this book, notably in his own broken romance in youth which left him with a sore heart for the rest of his life. He was not merely a dual personality; he was one of the most complex men who ever lived.

The history of Edinburgh, as indeed of all Scotland, is not of humankind and human things only. Other worlds are never entirely lost to sight and hearing.

1 St Margaret and St Giles

Edinburgh can hardly be called a city of saints. Sinners appear more frequently in her annals, including one of the blackest, the warlock Major Weir, but there is some holiness in her tradition, in her patron, St Giles, and in a queen and a king, St Margaret and King David I.

Of St Giles (or Aegidius) little is known. There was a cult of his sanctity in the Middle Ages, especially in Provence, round St-Giles and Arles. He is thought to have lived in the Dark Ages, before the ninth century. The legend is that he was a holy hermit, living in the woods, his only companion a white hind. One day Wamba, King of the Visigoths, rode hunting with his hounds in full cry. He fired an arrow at the hind, the swift creature fled into the undergrowth, and the arrow flew there. The hounds rushed in for the kill, and the King followed. He found Giles seated with the hind sheltered in his arms, the arrow stuck in the ground and the hounds transfixed by some strange power. The saint's emblem is an arrow; his day is 1 September.

About Margaret, queen and saint, much more is known. She came to her kingdom of Scotland as a refugee, married King Malcolm and reigned over the hearts and minds of her people. She was loving and gentle, strong and compassionate, caring for the poor and bringing grace and gentle manners into the royal household. Much of her time and Malcolm's was spent in Dunfermline, but when the King and his two eldest sons rode into Northumberland to fight the English, Margaret was in Edinburgh, in the castle on the rock. There she had an oratory, a tiny chapel where she prayed and heard Mass. Edinburgh was the best place for her to be: it is nearer the Border than Dunfermline, and from the high castle messengers from England could be seen far off.

In her delightful history of *Royal Edinburgh* Mrs Oliphant (herself named Margaret) tells us that it was known as 'the Castle of the Maidens': 'It is strange, yet scarcely difficult to the imagination to realise the embodiment of what is now Edinburgh in the far distance of the early ages . . . in the days when the king's daughters, primitive princesses with their rude surroundings were placed for safety in the *castrum puellarum*, the maiden castle, a title in after days proudly (but perhaps not very justly) adapted to the supposed invulnerability of the fortress perched upon its rock.' 'Embodiment' is just the word. The castle holds the essence of Edinburgh's tradition, history and character. The mists of legend may drift about the rock and its fortress but the strong foundations and building are there.

Queen Margaret came sad, anxious and ill to wait and pray. She prayed and heard Mass in the 'little sanctuary, plain and bare as a shed', as Margaret Oliphant describes it, calling it the 'oldest relic in Edinburgh.' The Queen held one still older relic and one of incomparable holiness. It was a fragment of black wood said to be a piece of the very cross of Christ itself. The Black Rood was enclosed in another cross of fine gold on which was carved in ivory a figure of the crucified Christ. The Queen had brought this with her to Scotland.

The Castle from the Vennel

Her last days were shadowed by foreboding: the King her husband would not return alive from his battle in Northumberland. It was true foresight. Her second son came with the news of his father's death and also that of his brother. Margaret heard this with unflinching fortitude: 'I thank Thee, Lord, that Thou givest me this agony to bear in my death hour.'

She asked for the Holy Rood. Holding it in her arms, she received Extreme Unction and died in peace. The King's body was brought back to Dunfermline, and hers was taken to be laid with his. Her lovely memory lives in the castle and in the tiny oratory on the site of the one where she worshipped, which is itself very old. It has been restored and is cherished by the people of Scotland, especially the Margarets.

She died on 16 November. At the Eucharist on that day there is read the passage from Proverbs describing the virtuous woman who looks well to the ways of her house, in whose tongue is the law of kindness, who feeds and clothes the poor.

Her son David continued the way of holiness. 'A sair sanct for the croun'* (as one of his successors, James I, was ruefully to call him), for his spending so much of the royal treasury on the founding of churches and abbeys. He founded Holyrood, Abbey of the Holy Cross. His legend has both a cross and a deer in it.

David continued his mother's ways of prayer and devotion, but he could lapse slightly. He went out hunting on Holy Cross Day, 14 September, when his confessor sternly told him he should have been at prayer in his oratory. He rode into the forest which lay close to the castle and what was then little more than a village or collection of huts. Suddenly he found himself separated from his companions and confronted by a great white stag with wide branching antlers. The creature, driven frantic by the noise of huntsmen and hounds, knocked the King from his horse. David rose and drew his sword to defend himself. Suddenly there shone a silver radiance, filling the sky. From the heart of this light came a hand holding a marvellous cross, which it handed to the King.

The stag fled and the King returned safely and devoutly to his oratory, there to give thanks to God. That night he had a dream of St Andrew, patron and guardian of Scotland. In the dream St Andrew bade him found an abbey of Augustinian friars to be dedicated to the Holy Rood.

The ruins of Holyrood Chapel

The arms of Edinburgh bear a shield with three crosses above a three-tiered castle, with on the right (dexter) side a maiden, on the left (sinister) side a white doe.

The seal of the city bears on one side a castle, on the other the figure of St Giles holding in one hand his crozier, in the other a book.

Sanctity and learning, castle of defence, lady and gentle doe are all part of the tradition.

Source
M. Oliphant, *Royal Edinburgh*

2 Châtelard and the Holyrood Tragedy

The Palace of the Kings (as a foreign visitor once called it), that rose beside the Abbey of the Holy Cross, has seen much drama, most of it tragic. The tragedy has come from human folly, from passion – some may think from the doom of the Stewarts. It has caught not only themselves but often their adherents, even, as in this tale of one coming unbidden, out of passionate desire and self-will. The story of Châtelard, poet and lover, is one of the most pitiful tragedies. His is a prelude to the greater and more complex tragedy of the queen he loved, Mary, Queen of Scots. It is the first of the shadows that fell across her path – the path from Holyrood to the block at Fotheringay.

It happened soon after she came from France, in 1561, to this grey city of preachers. She was young and lovely, gentle and courteous, worthy of love. An unselfish love might have saved her and given her long life and a happy reign, but that defence was withheld.

Châtelard was a poet, young, gifted and ardent – too ardent for his own good, or for the Queen's. He came from France, as Mary herself had done, to the port of Leith, thence to the city, and to the Canongate, the street of the canons of the abbey, though no longer was there an abbey as a place of worship, and there were no canons serving choir and altar. Master John Knox and his followers had great power, people flocked to hear him in the kirk of St Giles up the way. The queen herself heard Mass, though it was sternly disapproved, in her chapel.

Châtelard came to an inn kept by one Goodall, took a room there and asked that supper be served him, with a bottle of wine. Goodall served him himself and was courteously asked to sit and drink a glass of wine with his guest, who spoke enough English to understand and be understood, although the speech of Edinburgh must have been strange to French ears. He spoke with friendliness and courtesy, and the innkeeper responded. His guest told him that he had been at the French Court and that he had had the honour of being presented to the young Queen

The Canongate looking west

before her widowhood. He spoke much of her beauty, her skill in music, her gentleness.

'Aye, she's bonny, I'll grant ye that. And she has a word and a smile for a. It's a peety she is a Papist and has the idolatry o the Mass in her chapel. She wad be better hearin the Word preached by Maister John Knox.'

Châtelard flushed a little, but he controlled his feeling of offence at this attack on his and the Queen's faith.

'Is she content here, your Queen so young and so lovely? Must she not long for France, her mother's country, once her kingdom?'

'I kenna what she feels, but she'll hae tae be content tae bide here.'

Goodall was beginning to tire of this talk. His guest was too eloquent. 'He fair deaved me,'* he told his wife later. 'He's near daft.' Presently he was able to withdraw. Châtelard bade him goodnight and asked to have paper, quills and ink sent into to him as he had a letter to write.

His host was not far wrong. This guest was in a state of emotion and excitement very near frenzy. His room was on the upper floor and he could be heard walking about, talking, chanting, to himself.

'Will he ne'er be quiet?', said Goodall.

At last there was silence and everyone went to bed.

In the morning Châtelard appeared, quiet and controlled. He handed the innkeeper a letter, a scroll tied with green ribbon and sealed. It was addressed to the Queen herself, at the Palace of Holyrood, and he asked that it be taken to her. Later that morning the innkeeper took it himself.

The Queen was in her apartments with her ladies, the four Maries who had been with her since her childhood and who together had followed her to France and then back to Scotland: Mary Beaton, Mary Seton, Mary Livingstone and Mary Fleming. There were two or three French ladies too, and French was much spoken.

A gentleman of the household brought the letter tied with its green ribbon. 'This has an air of France,' said Mary. She opened it, read it and laughed.

'Can you guess who has sent this?' she asked one of her French maids. 'Try, I beg you.'

The girl suggested two or three names of young nobles, known to be devoted to the Queen.

Holyrood Palace

'No, it is none of these. It is – can you believe it? – young Châtelard. He has sent me a poem. Take it, and read it to us.'

The poem was a passionate hymn of love and praise, almost of worship. Mary and her ladies laughed a little, but very kindly. There had been nothing like this in the long weeks since their coming to Edinburgh.

'There's a letter too,' the Queen told them. 'He implores me to receive him. He is indeed reckless and passionate, but what would you – he is a poet of a fine talent, and these poets are not as other men. Moreover, he is of good family, known at the French Court. His extravagance does not altogether please me, but it would be better to receive him than to dismiss. We cannot have him wandering about the town reciting his poems, or declaiming them in a tavern.'

Her ladies agreed. They were indeed glad of this return of gallantry, which was sadly lacking in that grey city; they longed for music other than the droning of psalms, which might be for edification but was hardly for delight. Mary then bade the gentleman go to the inn, taking a page with him, and bid Monsieur Châtelard come to her. A room must be prepared for him in the palace.

Châtelard received the bidding with a rapture that was intensified by the gracious welcome he received. The Queen spoke to him in French, and she bade her ladies welcome him, which they did very willingly. His behaviour was immaculate: he was deferential to the Queen and courteous to her ladies. He had himself well in hand.

Mary may have had a shadow of foreboding, of the danger that might come from this worshipper, as indeed he was. But he was so gentle, so aware of her royal blood, and she so longed for the sweetness of France. There was little of *la douceur de vie* in the city of John Knox and his adherents.

'I thank you for your poem, Monsieur Châtelard, and for the air of France you bring, and so do my ladies. Now you will wish to retire, and to rest a little. We would gladly see you again this evening, perhaps hear another poem, talk again of France.'

The poet bowed and withdrew. He was escorted to the room prepared for him, and a servant came to ask if he desired anything. Châtelard fell into a dream from which he emerged to compose another poem. It spoke of the ineffable beauty and grace of the Queen, of his love for her. It was a fine poem but it began to come dangerously near to ecstasy. He recited, he declaimed, he chanted the lines. The servant heard, laughed and summoned others, who crowded round the door. This was as good as a play, an entertainment which they found dismally lacking in Edinburgh. They could understand not one word, but the meaning was made clear by the fervour of the speaker. They listened, laughed and made crude comments.

'Och, thae Frenchies! A daft lot.'

'The puir chiel's fair gyte.'*

'Aye, but he has a bonnie voice.'

Then one of them whispered, 'Wheesht! See wha's comin,' and they fled in a huddle.

The newcomer was formidable, no less a person than the Queen's half-brother, the Earl of Moray, the bastard son of her father, James V. There were some, especially Moray himself, who thought he should have been king. He was a good Protestant with no French and Popish devilment in him. He stood glowering at the retreating herd and called to one of them, 'Johnstone, come here to me.'

Johnstone obeyed.

'Whit gaes on here?' demanded Moray. 'Wha's in that room?'

'It's a daft loon o a Frenchman, my lord, sent for by the Queen a whilie syne,* an weel received. She bade this room be prepared for him. He's been there recitin an singin like a daftie.'

Moray nodded, dismissed the man and stood at the door. He understood French and he heard the rapturous effusion of the poet. He then walked away and came upon the chamberlain of the household.

'Who is the French fellow whom Her Grace has received, who now occupies a room?'

'His name is Châtelard, my lord. He sent a letter to Her Grace this morning and she had him brought here, and into her presence. Then she ordered a room to be prepared for him. He is, it appears, a poet.'

Moray laughed grimly.

'Aye, he thinks himself that. I've heard of him – a silly rhymster and jingler, such as thae hae aboot the French court.'

He walked away well pleased. The Queen's impetuous act might prove to his profit and be a weapon against her – a weapon which this bitter and jealous brother would store up with any more that might come to hand. Châtelard's passion was very obvious, already inspiring gossip among the servants, who would carry it beyond the palace – gossip welcomed by many who looked doubtfully upon their young and lovely Queen, because of her frivolity, as they considered it, and because of her adherence to the old Catholic faith. Many of her people loved her, captivated by her beauty, charm and friendliness, but even they might in time be won away from her. If she were indiscreet, if she were to show the faintest approach to returning Châtelard's passion – then there might be a great fall.

Meanwhile Moray kept a silence which was malicious rather than loyal. The Queen's ladies were less discreet. They chattered about this charming young poet, about his delightful verses. The gossip spread, mingling with that from the servants.

That evening the Queen sent again for Châtelard. His coming had brought new life. She loved to hear news of France, to speak French, to listen to poetry and songs. Her ladies shared the pleasure. She was very gracious, and the infatuated poet began to dream of a return of his love.

Moray was aware of this. He had uttered no rebuke. There was no need of one. The danger to the Queen through gossip and scandal would flourish without any encouragement from him. But he took his own measures. He summoned one of the French servants, Choisseul, whom he had rightly judged to be corruptible; he was a man always in need of money.

To him Moray spoke benevolently.

'You speak and understand a little of our language?'

'I do, my lord.'

'You would like perhaps to earn a little money?'

'Indeed, my lord, your lordship is most gracious and most understanding.'

'You have seen this Frenchman? You have heard the gossip? I believe he intends to harm Her Grace.' Moray was now the affectionate and loyal brother, gravely concerned for his sister's safety.

'This Châtelard may appear a harmless poor fool of a fellow, but he is crafty. Keep your ears and eyes open. He will never suspect you. You alone can do this, and you will not go unrewarded.' He slipped a purse into the ready hand of Choisseul, who bowed deeply.

'My lord, you are too good, you are indeed my benefactor. I will serve you faithfully.'

Moray had chosen well. Choisseul had no great position and was not of much importance. He was an amiable fellow, but no one took him seriously. He absorbed a good deal, and he brought reports to Moray, who was well pleased.

Listening at Châtelard's door, the spy heard his ravings of passion, sometimes his declarations to himself that the Queen looked upon him with favour, with love. The fits of self-delusion were growing more frequent.

One night Mary came to her bedroom attended by two of her ladies. From inside a large aumry or cupboard where some of her dresses hung came sounds. The ladies would have called for help but the Queen forbade it.

'Let us see for ourselves, and only for ourselves, what this is.' She opened the door of the aumry. There stood Châtelard, with drawn sword, ready to defend himself. When he saw the Queen, he flung the sword to the ground, knelt down and clutched her skirt. Mary stood very still, very regal.

'What does this mean, Monsieur Châtelard? How dare you invade my privacy! Loose your hand, rise, and go. I could have you seized by the guard, taken to prison and thence . . .'

That was enough. Châtelard rose, his frenzy gone, and stood humbly with bowed head. He knew how she might have ended the sentence: '. . . thence to execution.'

'Forgive me, my Queen. I have indeed sinned, but by folly, not by treachery, only by your great love.'

'Silence! You will depart at once. Tomorrow you will leave the palace and, as soon thereafter as possible, my city and kingdom.'

He retired from the room silently, head bowed.

'There must be no talk of this,' the Queen commanded her ladies, who vowed they would be silent. They kept their word. They were loyal and discreet, knowing what disaster would come if anything were known of this episode – disaster not only for the wretched poet but also for the Queen.

Next morning Châtelard departed. There was no further talk. Choisseul for once had nothing to carry to Moray. The Queen and her immediate household were leaving Edinburgh on a tour of the northern part of her kingdom. She was moving first to Dunfermline for a night, thence to Burntisland and then to St Andrews. It was taken for granted that 'this poet fellow' should have left before her. If the servants and others thought of him at all, they supposed that he had gone back to France where they bred daft rhymsters and jinglers like him.

Mary, having stayed a night in Dunfermline, in the home of St Margaret (did she invoke her prayers and help?), continued her progress to Burntisland, where she spent the day hunting, a sport she loved. She returned to her lodging healthily tired and went early to her room unattended. As she sat down for a moment of solitude and silence, the door was flung open and Châtelard rushed in, falling on his knees before her.

'My Queen, my beloved, forgive me and listen. I cannot leave your kingdom and go into exile without your pardon, without your blessing, without a word of kindness from you. Listen, I implore you, to your most unhappy lover.'

'Sir! This is beyond pardon! Rise, and go at once, and be thankful I do not summon the guard to seize you.'

The Queen rose, a figure of terrible dignity. Châtelard knelt, sobbing, beside himself. The door was once again flung open, and the Earl of Moray strode in. Choisseul had done his work this time. He had kept watch on Châtelard at the inn, to which he had returned, and could report to his master that, instead of taking ship for France, the fugitive had crossed the Forth and followed the Queen. He had known her plans.

Moray stood looking on as Châtelard struggled to his feet.

'Well, sir poet, what does this mean? By whose leave, at whose bidding have you come?'

The frenzy left Châtelard. He spoke with dignity. 'I have come to bid farewell to Her Grace, before, in obedience to her command, I depart from her kingdom.'

'What have you to say, madam?' continued Moray, turning to the Queen who held herself rigid.

'There is no need to say more. It is as Monsieur Châtelard has said. Now let him depart.'

'Depart he shall – but not alone or free.'

Moray opened the door, called to an attendant and ordered him to bring the captain of the guard and another with him. Châtelard stood very still. The guard appeared.

'Take this fellow,' Moray ordered, 'and keep him closely confined.'

Châtelard made no resistance. He was led from the room. Moray turned to the Queen.

'Madam, you are safe for tonight, and I take it upon me to assure you that you are henceforth safe from that wretched rhymster.'

Mary looked at him beseechingly. She spoke gently.

'Brother, be merciful. He can do me no more harm.'

'He has done enough already. This night's work will do more. I cannot guard you from slander.'

'Surely he need not suffer death. You cannot intend that. Let him be banished. Indeed I myself commanded him to leave my kingdom. Let him go!'

'No doubt you have your own reasons for desiring him to live.' Moray spoke harshly, with a bitter sneer. 'It is not for me to judge. It is for the Privy Council.' He walked out of the room to his own apartments, where Choisseul awaited him.

'You have done well, very well,' Moray told him. 'Take this with my thanks.' He gave the spy a purse. There was gold in it. Choisseul bowed and thanked him profusely. Moray dismissed him and sat down to write letters which would be sent to the members of the Privy Council and to some of the Lords of Session, the chief lawyers in the kingdom.

These letters gave Moray's account of Châtelard's actions, of his being held captive, and they commanded the recipients to meet in judgement at St Andrews.

Next day the Queen and her retinue made their journey there, Moray among them. Châtelard was brought under close guard to prison there. On the following day the Privy Council and the law lords arrived and met as a court of judgement in the old castle.

There they sat, there the prisoner was brought, there Moray addressed Châtelard, with apparent impartiality, bidding him plead his own defence, without respect of the persons involved, however exalted. It was a thinly veiled injunction to accuse the Queen of encouraging him of complicity. Châtelard refused to play this ignoble part. He took the whole burden of folly upon himself, he denying any blacker guilt.

'Love compelled me. For her, that peerless lady and princess I would gladly die – die many deaths. I am guilty of folly, of too great love, but of nothing more. She is absolutely pure and guiltless.'

Again Moray urged him to defend himself, again Châtelard refused, again he declared that he alone had erred and his only crime was that of loving too deeply.

There was no more to be said. The court condemned him to be beheaded on the following day, 2 February 1563, Candlemas.

The Queen wept bitterly. Again she pleaded with her implacable brother – let Châtelard be banished, never to return to Scotland under pain of death – only let him live.

'That would be fatal to your honour,' Moray told her. 'Only his death will kill the scandal and slander.'

Moray's evil work was not finished. He sent again for Choisseul, to whom he spoke benignly.

'You have done excellently well, my friend. Will you do me a further small service?'

'I am at your lordship's command, now and always.'

'Then go to the prisoner in his cell. Here is a pass to admit you. Speak to him with compassion, as a friend who grieves for his fate, as a fellow Frenchman who would bid him farewell. Then suggest to him a way of escape. He may yet be spared. Let him declare that he is not alone in his guilt. Tell him you have reason to think that if he does so he will be released, his return to France made safe. You understand?'

'I understand perfectly, my lord, and I obey.'

Choisseul went that night to the cell where Châtelard lay. The prisoner greeted him quietly, responded quietly to his sympathy. Then Choisseul spoke softly and insinuatingly.

'Dear Monsieur Châtelard, you are not altogether guilty, not alone in your fault. That is understood. You have been the victim of someone exalted in rank who will, you think, grieve for you. But what is that worth? A woman's tears are soon dried. She will forget you. But if you should let it be known that she loved you and showed you her love and thus shares your guilt – then I think you may be set free; no questions will be asked, you will find yourself not on the scaffold but on the soil of France again.'

Châtelard rose. 'You ask me to accuse her, to be false to her, the purest of women. She is beyond reproach. I would rather die a hundred deaths. Leave me, you liar, you traitor!'

Châtelard in his fury would have killed the ignoble tempter. Choisseul escaped, went to Moray and made his report – which may have disappointed that master of craft but did not greatly surprise him.

Next morning Châtelard was led to the scaffold. Before he knelt to lay his head on the block, he recited a poem by his fellow-poet, Ronsard, his 'Hymn to Death.' Then he called, 'Farewell, most lovely and most cruel Princess.' Then he knelt down and laid his head on the block. He died with courage and with dignity as his beloved Princess was to die also in the month of February, twenty-four years later, after a captivity much longer than his.

Source
John Mackay Wilson: *Tales of the Borders*

3   The Fairy Boy of Leith

The Fairy Boy of Leith was a drummer. He played for the elves of Edinburgh who used to meet for feasting and dancing once a week, under the Calton Hill which is at the east end of Edinburgh, convenient to the port of Leith. He told a man all about it, and this man set it down in writing, having heard about the boy from a decent woman who kept a wine shop in Leith. It was a good shop where friends could meet and talk and drink, as they chose, ale or wine. They were wise if they chose wine, for at the port of Leith fine claret and burgundy came in from France.

The man – Burton was his name – listened while he drank a glass.

'He whiles come in,' the woman said, 'and he'll rin an errand for me. See, there he is,' as she looked out of the window. 'He's just run by.'

Burton rose and looked out. He saw a boy, about ten years old, run along and join two or three others at a game. At once he went out, went up to the boys, spoke to this particular one and asked him to come back with him to the wine shop.

'I want tae ask ye something. Maybe there will be a bawbee or twa in it.'*

The boy, a good-looking child, clean and neat, came with him. He spoke well, in a very clear, musical voice and with a subtlety beyond that of ordinary boys. As he spoke, he drummed on the table with his fingers, and it was a tune he drummed. He was very matter-of-fact, talking of his tryst with those other people as if they were some of the gentry in a big house.

'What is it like under the hill?' asked Burton. 'Is it cauld and dark?'

'Och no! It's a fine, big ha,* as grand as in Holyrood Palace itsel.' There was a wee door in the hillside which none knew but the little people themselves and those they summoned. It led into a hall hung with tapestries, lit by hundreds of candles. The only mortals who could enter were those who were partly of fairy blood or had their eyes touched and their sight quickened by

Exchange buildings, Leith

elfin fingers. The boy did not say if he had this blood in him, and Burton discreetly did not ask. It is not wise to ask too many questions, nor did he ask whether the boy was paid for his playing.

They met, these other people, always on a Thursday, at dusk, and they danced and feasted until daybreak on Friday. Their dancing was the most graceful ever seen, beyond even that of the late seventeenth-century fine ladies at balls and assemblies; the food and wine were rich and rare – none of your porridge and milk, bannocks* and cheese, but the finest white bread, cakes and marzipan confections and wines. You could eat and drink your fill and yet never feel heavy and drunken.

'Can ye tell fortunes?' asked Burton. 'Can ye see intae the future? Can ye see mine?'

'I can, easy. I can tell ye ye're no mairrit,* by ye will be. Ye'll hae twa wives, for the first will die young. They will baith be bonny and kind.'

The boy said he saw them clearly, one on each side of the man. Burton would have asked more questions, but the woman of the house came in.

Edinburgh from Calton Hill

'There's a neighbour here, speirin* for ye,' she told the boy, 'She wants ye tae tell her future.'

The neighbour came into the room, and the boy looked at her.

'I see ye had twa bairns afore ye mairrit ye're man. He's no the faither o either o them,' he told her, much to her confusion. It was her future she wanted to know, not her past. She turned and ran out of the room, out of the house and down the road. Fortunately the wine-shop keeper was discreet. She had heard many a tale when her customers had drunk that extra glass and had never spoken a word or let on she had heard. That was one reason, along with her good manners and her good wine, why so many customers came.

'Save us a,' she said now. 'Wha wad hae thocht it? She's aye sae prim!'

The man gave the boy a silver piece and told him to come again. The boy ran off to play with his friends, the man paid his lawing* and bade his hostess goodnight. He told some of his friends about the boy. Some believed him, some were sceptical. Burton himself was more fascinated than he had been since he was a boy and had heard tales from his granny of those 'other people.' He invited some of his friends to come with him to the wine shop. The boy was in the street, and he came in with them willingly enough. Burton bade him sit down in the middle of their group, himself on one side, another man on the other, someone behind him. Again the boy spoke clearly, again drumming a tune on the table, and he answered their questions politely.

Och yes, the elves were bonny folk, men and women. They were small and light of foot, dancing like a wave of the sea. They were most elegantly dressed in delicate silks of lovely colours, or in silver and gold, with jewels. They ate and drank moderately, they talked and laughed, they listened to music, then danced again until daybreak, when they all streamed out of the door in the hill and away – where the boy could not or would not say.

Then suddenly one of the guests asked, 'Whaur is he, the laddie?'

'I didna see him gang,' said another. 'Did he open the door or slip oot by the windae?'

Burton went out, ran from the house and saw the wee boy in

the street. 'Come back, laddie,' he said, 'an ye'll hae cake an a glass o wine an a siller piece.'*

The boy came back, ate a little, drank a little – then suddenly he was off again, none of them could tell exactly how.

Burton again ran out. He saw the boy flying along the road towards Edinburgh, towards the Calton Hill. He caught up with him and took hold of him by the arm.

'Where awa, laddie? Come back and tell us mair.' But the boy sent up a wild cry, that he was being attacked. It would have brought the watch down on them, and Burton would have looked exceedingly foolish, which he did not care to do, so he let the boy go and returned ruefully to his companions. They drank another glass together as they talked about the boy and his strange tale of the elfin dances within the hill.

They were douce, sensible men all of them, not given to strange imaginings. Having drunk well but not deeply, they paid their lawing, adding a silver piece for the boy should he come back. The good wife would give it to him. She might, Burton hoped, have some news for him next time he called.

But never again did he or any of his friends see or hear of the Fairy Boy again. Whether he continued to be drummer to the elves when they gathered to dance in their hall beneath the Calton Hill, whether they draw him into their company for all time, whether he was partly of their blood, was never known. He lives in legend and, it may be, within the Calton Hill.

Source
Sir Walter Scott: *Minstrelsy of the Scottish Border*

4   The Good Neighbour

It is a fine thing both to be and to have a good neighbour, especially if the latter is a Good Neighbour in the old sense – one of the Good People, the name respectfully given to the fairies, the 'other people,' by way of propitiation, precaution and courtesy. Sir Godfrey Maccullough, a late seventeenth-century Galloway laird, discovered this.

Walking near his house one morning, he met a little old man he had not seen before, who stopped and desired to speak with him. The laird greeted him in his usual friendly way and asked where he lived.

'Doun below ye're ain hoose, below the kitchen and cellars. It was a fine dwelling until noo, and I've been weel content, but the drains and sewers are lettin their filth intae the hoose, intae my but and ben,* and there's nocht I can do.'

'I am indeed sorry to hear that,' Sir Godfrey replied. 'It shall be dealt with at once. I shall send for the workman now.'

'Thank ye. Gude day tae ye, laird! Ye're a gude neighbour,' said the little man and disappeared.

Sir Godfrey acted at once. He sent his men to clear and repair the drains, to wash away the flood of the filth and to leave everything decent. Then he thought no more about the matter.

He was indeed a good neighbour, a good laird and master, much liked by his friends. He was kind-hearted, generous and approachable. But he had one fault: he had a quick temper which could too easily flare into rage. This was his undoing.

A quarrel with an acquaintance led to a duel in which the other man was killed – which of them was more to blame was not decided. Sir Godfrey was arrested, tried and condemned to be executed. He was imprisoned in Edinburgh, and the scaffold was set up on the Castle Hill. No plea was made, no attempt to escape.

On the morning of the execution a crowd gathered near the scaffold. The executioner stood by the block, leaning on his axe.

The Castle from the Mound

Sir Godfrey arrived, walking between two guards, not bound or manacled. People looked on him with compassion.

Then, suddenly, there was the sound of hooves. A white horse came through the streets up the hill, swift as the wind. His rider was a little old man. He stopped beside the prisoner.

'Mount behind me, Sir Godfrey,' and Sir Godfrey, recognizing him, obeyed. He leapt up behind the rider, the horse rushed off again down the hill through the streets, swift as the wind, none trying or wishing to obstruct him and his riders. None of the three was ever seen again.

So it is as well to be and to have a good neighbour.

Source
Sir Walter Scott, *Minstrelsy of the Scottish Border*

5   The Confession of Mary Hamilton

> Last night the Queen had four Maries,
> The night she'll hae but three;
> There was Mary Seaton and Mary Beaton
> And Mary Carmichael an me.

The story or confession of Mary Hamilton, part-told by herself, is one of the most tragic of Scottish ballads, but the historian asks if Mary Hamilton and Mary Carmichael were really part of the quartet. The real four Maries were Mary Seaton, Mary Beaton, Mary Livingstone and Mary Fleming.

But Mary Hamilton lives in that ballad, lives in legend. It may have been propaganda in the campaign against the Queen. A ballad is circulated, it is said or sung by the multitude, the rhyme and rhythm are haunting and unforgettable.

The King, Darnley, saw her, fell in love and seduced her. Or did she deliberately seduce him – to pay for it in her bitter death?

> Marie Hamilton's to the kirk gane,
> Wi ribbons in her hair;
> The King thoucht mair o Marie Hamilton
> Than ony that were there.
>
> Marie Hamilton's to the kirk gane,
> Wi ribbons on her briest.
> The King thoucht mair o Marie Hamilton
> Than he listened to the priest.

It is a very Scottish setting – that first look of love and loss of heart – not at a Court ball or any feast but in the kirk. She was a bonny lass; she knew it and made the most of it. The King had a roving glance with never a thought for his wife, the Queen.

View of the old town and St Giles

The King thocht mair o Marie Hamilton
Than the Queen and a her lands
And soon his desire compelled her, and
Frae the King's Court Marie Hamilton,
Marie Hamilton daurna* be.

So it went on until she was with child and dared not admit it. The
King tried and failed in a sinful way of escape for her:

The King is to the Abbey gane
To pu the Abbey tree,
To scale the babe frae Marie's heart
But the thing it wadna be.

And so the babe was born and had no welcome:

O she has rowed it in her apron
And set it on the sea.
'Gae sink ye, or swim ye, bonny babe,
Ye'se get nae mair o me.'

But Mary would 'get mair o the bonny babe'. Though the tiny body sank, the cruel story swam and came to shore. Edinburgh was and is a thriving place for gossip, and within the microcosm of the Queen's Court the scandal flourished.

> Word is to the kitchen gane
> And word is to the ha
> And word is to the noble room
> Amang the ladies a
> That Marie Hamilton's brought to bed
> And the bonny bairn's missed and awa.

She had crept back to bed and lain down but scarcely fallen asleep when

> Up and started our gude Queen
> Just at her bed-feet

demanding where was the bonny babe, 'For I'm sure I heard it greet.' But Mary protested it was not so, it could not be so. She herself had cried out in pain.

> Was but a stotch into my side,
> and sair it troubles me.

But the Queen believed no such tale. She commanded Mary to rise and follow her, to ride into Edinburgh to a wedding. Mary must obey: she must dress and mount her horse and ride with her mistress.

> Slowly rade she out the way
> Wi mony a weary groan.
>
> The Queen was clad in scarlet,
> Her ladies all in green.
> In every town they came to
> They took Marie Hamilton for the Queen.

(And whence they rode and through what towns the ballad does not say and we need not ask.)

She implored her companions to 'ride hooly, hooly' (slowly

The Canongate Tolbooth

and gently) for never had 'a wearier burd rade in your company' than herself so lately in childbed, from which she had risen first to lay her babe on the sea and next to ride with the Queen, her implacable mistress. For Queen Mary, whom the four Maries must attend, was jealous, vengeful, implacable, and a dreadful fate awaited Mary Hamilton.

The news had spread. The women who stood to see the cavalcade were weeping in pity, and Mary Hamilton cried to them or to herself.

> Why weep ye sae, ye burgess wives,
> Why look ye sae on me?
> O I am going to Edinburgh town
> A rich wedding to see.

But they came to no church or palace. They came to the Tolbooth stairs.

> And lang or e'er she cam doon again
> She was condemned to die

Then she came to the Netherbow, and there she laughed 'loud laughters tree,' and so to the gallows foot and 'the tears blinded her ee.' And there she spoke her lament, her valediction.

> Yestreen the Queen had four Maries.
> This night she'll hae but three.
> There was Mary Seaton and Mary Beaton
> And Mary Carmichael and me.

She had served the Queen and dressed her and put gold into her hair,

> But now I've gotten for my reward
> The gallows to be my share.

She had waited upon the Queen and often made her bed,

> But now I've gotten to my reward
> The gallows tree to tread.

Her mother and father were far away. They must not know her fate.

> I charge ye all, ye mariners
> That sail upon the foam,
> Let neither my father nor mother get wit
> But that I'm coming home.

Let them live in hope and expectancy and in ignorance.

> May neither my mother nor father get wit
> the dog's death I'm to die

For if they do, they and her brothers three

> O muckle wad be the gude red blude
> This day wad be spilt for me.

And so, at the gallows foot her final lament:

> Little did my mither ken
> The day she cradled me,
> The lands I was to travel in
> Or the death I wis to die.

The voice is haunting. Did she see it then? A tiny newborn babe, wrapped in an apron, laid on the sea.

Source
F. J. Child, *The English and Scottish Popular Ballads*, Vol. 3, p. 379

6   The Monk and the Innkeeper

Drink and religion may meet in amity if both are genial without being excessive. But there may be a touch of trickery if there has been excess, as happened in this story of the monk and the innkeeper in Leith, at the time when the Reformation had begun to take over and to threaten the Catholic faithful, especially the clergy.

The young Mary, Queen of Scots, had been sent to France by her wise mother, Mary of Guise, who was now Regent of a disturbed country and city. She had her palace in Leith. At this moment the town was under attack by the Lords of the Congregation and their English allies and was defended by French troops sent to help the Queen Regent. The monks of St Anthony had their small monastery in the Kirkgate, whence they came, as unobtrusively as possible, to visit the faithful who desired their help, and some who had no particular spiritual needs, though of good and genial enough character.

Among the latter was Davie Wemyss, landlord of the Ship Inn, which was much frequented by those who knew good wine. His cellar was well supplied with what one is tempted to call that good Scots drink, claret, so much was the wine of Bordeaux enjoyed in Edinburgh. A supply had just been delivered to the Ship Inn, and Davie was happily employed in tapping a hogshead when he heard a gentle knock on a back door, near the cellar, a door known to customers who might prefer to make their visits unobtrusive or who came on business. It might, Davie thought, be the skipper of the *The Cut-Luggit* * *Sow*, or Willie the herring-curer. He went to the door and opened it – to a monk well known to him, in a long black habit and a black shovel hat.

'It's yersel, Faither Peter. Come awa in. I'll let ye taste the claret just come frae Bordeaux. Ye're a gude judge.'

Father Peter Drinkhooley, as he was not unsuitably called, came in and was conducted to the small back room where Davie did much of his business, and served with a generous tankard of the benign drink.

'It is gude wine, David my son, mellow. Is it a large cask?'

'Big eneuch* tae last oot the siege, I hope.'

'Indeed, these are evil times. The heretics are strong. But the day will come when they will be scattered like chaff. There has been a great slaughter this very day. I come from giving the last rites to two brave officers. They made a good ending, and they left me gifts for our monastery. We need it. See – the one gave me 150 crowns, the other three bonny gold rings.' He drew two little bags out from a pocket. 'Good men and faithful. May they rest in peace.'

'Amen,' said Davie.

Father Peter drank again, more than one draught.

'Faith, it is good wine, Davie.'

He looked thoughtfully into the tankard. Davie, a generous man, took the hint – 'Ye'll can dae wi a drap mair, Faither?' – and took the empty tankard, bringing it back well filled. He had not drained his own. He was a prudent drinker, knowing the exact strength of his head. It is not wise for the vintner to exceed his limit. Father Peter drank again. Slowly he came to the last drop and set down the tankard.

'It has been a hard day and a trying one, David. I could do with a sleep before I go back.'

'Aye, ye'd be the better o it. Come ben, Faither, there's a wee room here wi a bed. Lay doun yer hat, tak aff the habit and lie doun. I'll wauken ye in twa hours an ye'll be back in the monastery in gude time.'

Father Peter obeyed. He laid his coat and habit aside, lay down and was asleep before Davie closed the door.

Davie himself, clear in head and steady of hand, continued his work, then went upstairs ready to serve his customers. There was a loud, frantic knocking at the front door. Davie opened it to find a boy, calling out frantically.

'A priest! A priest! Wull ye send fir yin noo? There's a Frenchman lyin oan the ramparts, sair woundit, like tae die, an he's greetin* oot fir a priest tae shrive him.'

'Ye need seek nae further,' Davie Wemyss told him. 'There's a monk here, in this hoose. He has been shrivin twa men already, he has lain doun fir a wee bit rest, but I'll rouse him.'

The boy ran off before Davie could stop him – but Father Peter would know where to go, he would find his penitent. Davie went

down to the little room and found the monk in such a deep slumber that there was little hope of rousing him.

'An little gude he wad dae if he were roused. I maun gang to the monastery and find anither.' Davie told himself. Then his eye fell on the habit and the shovel hat. Temptation took hold of him as he remembered the priest's gold from other dying men.

'Whit wey no?' he asked himself. 'I could pass for a priest in that priestly garb. I ken whit tae say. It wad be a charity to the puir soul in need.'

His mind was made up. He put on the habit, set the wide hat on his head, let himself out by the back door into a narrow alley and proceeded quickly and quietly towards the ramparts. Suddenly he was stopped by a hand on his shoulder and a voice that spoke courteously but with authority.

'Good father, come with me at once. A dying woman needs help. I have promised to bring her the first priest I should meet.'

'But I canna gang wi you. I'm on my wey tae a dyin man,' protested Davie. His arm was taken by a firm hand; the voice spoke again with authority.

'You will be conducted to wherever you would go – but after you have come with me and done your office. Now come, and do not make me compel you.'

'But ye wadna dae that tae a priest and monk.'

'I hope not, but if you resist, I shall. You are in no danger. You will be brought back safely and well rewarded.' Davie thought of those gold rings and the bag of coins that had been given to Father Peter.

The stranger gave a low whistle. Two armed men appeared from a dark close and stood one on either side of him.

'Follow me,' said his captor, walking away, followed by the now reluctant bogus monk held gently but firmly between two other men. Davie decided to confess his trickery and called out to his captor.

'Bide a wee, sir. I'm no a monk, I'm no a priest. I'm Davie Wemyss wha keeps the Ship Inn.'

'So you say. I can forgive your attempt to escape. Times are not easy for us Catholics, especially for the clergy. But it would be less safe for you to try to escape now. I have never heard of Davie Wemyss whose name you have taken. I am under strict orders to bring a priest and I shall do so.'

He walked on. Davie followed between his two warders.

'Ye maun ken me,' he said. 'Ye maun ken the Ship Inn.'

But one man muttered, 'No Engleesh;' the other shook his head. They came to the Water of Leith, to the closely guarded bridge and ramparts. The mysterious leader spoke a word or two in French, and the gate was opened. The guard made an obeisance to the supposed priest, and the little group passed through. A little further on they found four horses saddled and waiting. Davie mounted very awkwardly and rode towards the city. The leader warned Davie to be very quiet and to draw no attention to himself. They rode down the back of the Canongate and were turning into the High Street when there was a yell from a mocker.

'Prelacy's mounted! Prelacy's mounted!' It came from a boy who soon had a following, shouting in mockery with more than an undertone of rage.

'Doun wi Popery, doun wi the man o sin in Rome, doun wi the limbs o Satan!'

'Spur on your horse and ride,' the leader told Davie. He set the example himself by galloping off, followed by the two guards. But Davie was no horseman.

Stock Bridge, Water of Leith

'Gude folk, I'm no a priest. I'm nae mair a monk than ony o yersels,' he called, but his voice was drowned in the shouts of 'Doun wi the papists! Doun wi the monks!' A stone hit him on the head. He fell from his horse among the yelling mob, unconscious.

Another voice spoke, a voice of authority, which matched the appearance of the speaker, a tall man of dignified bearing, carrying a sword.

'Cowards and villains, spoilers of the Church. Will you add sacrilege to your crimes?' He thrust about him with his sword. More than one felt a cut. More, however, than any stroke, his voice and bearing subdued them. There was, moreover, a certain shame. Their victim might die. They had not intended that. It would bring trouble.

'Ten crowns to any man who will carry this poor victim of your cruelty whither I shall direct you.' There was a moment of silence. Then a great brawny fellow in a smith's leather apron stepped forward.

'I'm yer man.' He turned to the crowd. 'Come on, Rab, and you Jock. Ten crown are worth the havin.' Two sturdy men came forward to pick up the unconscious figure.

'Stop!' commanded the rescuer. 'You cannot take hold of him as if he were a dead dog. Fetch a stretcher or a litter. Another crown for that.' They found one, a rough affair of boards, but it served. Poor battered Davie was laid on it, still unconscious, and carried off after his rescuer.

Back at the Ship Inn, Father Peter Drinkhooley came gradually to the surface, refreshed and clear in mind, suffering not at all after his excesses. He sat up, reached for his habit and found none. Habit and hat were gone. He must find them, put them on and be off to the monastery before the gate was closed. First he must find David his host. But the door was locked. He knocked and called out, quietly, then louder. The door was opened, and there stood not Davie but his wife.

'Good Mistress Wemyss,' said the monk, 'can ye call David? I cannot find my habit and my hat, and I cannot go back like this.'

'Indeed, Reverend Faither, I canna find Davie masel. I cam tae see if he were here. I havena seen him since he cam doun tae the cellar here tae draw some o the new claret. They tell me a laddie

cam to the street door a while back and they heard him an Davie colloguin.* Goad send him safe back. He's been awa three hours an mair.'

In dismay and bewilderment Father Peter searched the little cell of a room. There was no sign of his monastic dress. He dared not wait any longer.

'Will you send your wee lass, Mistress Wemyss, to the monastery to tell Brother Christie that I came here for a word with my good friend David Wemyss, that I was wearied after my visits to the poor dying men and fell asleep, and that I cannot find my habit. She is to ask him to let her have another to bring to me.'

'Aye, Jeannie will gang,' agreed kind Mrs Wemyss. Jeannie ran off and came back very soon without habit or hat.

'Brither Christie says ye maun come as ye are. He says ye maun hae drunk owre muckle o ma faither's new claret,' which showed Brother Christie's perceptiveness.

'I'll lend ye a coat an hat o Davie's,' said Mrs Wemyss comfortingly.

Thus decently clad in lay garb, the monk slipped out by the back door, and by dark alleys and side streets he aimed at the monastery, where the door was opened to him by Brother Christie with some caustic comments – but also with the reassuring advice to go to his cell and maybe the proper garb would be found there.

To return to poor Davie, he came to himself lying on a wide, soft bed, hung with tapestry, covered with fine linen sheets and velvet, a bed fit for a king and in a room large and grand like the bed. He lay for a few minutes, still dazed and bewildered. Gradually his mind cleared. He sat up and looked about him. This was obviously a household of the old religion. Over the fireplace hung a large painting of the Crucifixion, on a table by the bed stood a silver crucifix, and before it a prie-dieu. He was further roused by a gentle knock on the door. A man came in, moving softly, carrying a silver bowl filled with a most fragrant posset. He approached the bed and spoke very respectfully.

'Reverend Father, I trust that you are recovered. Will you drink this posset, made from a prescription of our own good doctor and made by her ladyship's own hands, my Lady Wisherton. It was her son, the young lord, who by happy

chance came on you and routed those villains and had you carried here.'

'Was it so? In troth, I'm muckle* obliged to his lordship and to her leddyship. Weel, let's try this posset.' Davie dipped, dipped again and drank a good draught. It was a rare mixture of more ingredients than he could first recognize, perfectly blended, savoury, and he was something of a connoisseur. His good wife was an excellent cook and had her own recipes, but this was something special. Slowly he drank it to the last drop.

'My thanks and compliments to her leddyship. That is the best posset I have ever tasted.'

'Her ladyship will be gratified.'

The man took the cup, bowed and went out, after wishing the patient a good night. Davie lay very comfortably. Again there came a soft knock on the door, and this time a lady entered: she was an elderly lady, tall, very dignified, handsome, dressed in black velvet with a lace ruff and cap, wearing a diamond cross on a gold chain round her neck. David began to sit up.

'Pray, Father, do not disturb yourself. You are in need of rest. I trust you begin to feel better?'

'Indeed I dae, yer leddyship, thank ye kindly, and thank ye for the posset which is the best I hae ever tasted.' He nearly said he would describe it to his wife but he recollected himself.

'It is our privilege and good fortune to have you with us, Father. My son sends his most respectful greetings.'

'Faith, I'm muckle indebted tae his lordship. He saved ma life.'

If the lady was somewhat surprised by the monk's mode of speech, she did not show it. She went on to speak with horror of the ruffians who had so brutally set about the good monk. Davie agreed heartily.

'But noo, thanks tae yer leddyship and that gude posset, I feel mysel recovered, an if yer leddyship will no think me ungratefu, I think I'd better be on my wey back tae the monastery.'

'But indeed you must not leave our house tonight. You are not yet fully recovered – as you may be in the morning. Rest now, good Father, and sleep, with a mind at ease. We have sent a message to St Anthony's that you will be with them in the morning, when my son himself will have the honour of escorting you.'

This was the worst shock of all, but to protest would not help.

He accepted her ladyship's decision with many thanks. She wished him a good night, with healing slumber, and withdrew.

At about midnight, when Davie's wife was sitting up awake, anxious and alert for any sound, there was a knock at that small back door. She opened it quickly and softly.

'Davie, my ain. Och, the lord be thankit and our Blessed Leddy! Whaur hae ye been? Come awa in, and lat me see tae ye.' She drew him in, made him sit by the fire and brought a cup of her own posset – which was nearly as good as her ladyship's.

'So it wis yersel as had Faither Peter's goun an hat!' For Davie had again donned the monk's hat and habit for his flight. He told her the whole story. She listened amazed, and with more admiration for her man's courage and resource than disapproval. She was proud of her Davie. Her gratitude to her ladyship and her son was profound.

Davie told how he had escaped. When all was quiet, he had left his fine room and come to a little room at the back of the house, one floor above the courtyard, and let himself carefully down; then he had stolen through the dark, by side streets and alleys – maybe not for the first time.

The next day he called at the monastery, bearing a peace-offering of good Bordeaux. It was accepted with proper gratitude and a blessing upon the donor. His apology for the mislaying of the habit and hat was also accepted. Indeed, it is doubtful whether any but Brother Christie knew or suspected much, if anything, about Father Peter's absence, and Brother Christie was a man of decency, humour and discretion.

Davie said nothing more about his adventure. But an innkeeper is not a remote person, and Edinburgh and Leith are full of long, alert ears and long, lively tongues. Something of the tale got around and produced a popular rhyme:

> Davie Wemyss gaed oot a priest,
> By filthy lucre tempted;
> Davie Wemyss cam hame again,
> An thocht naebody kent it.*

Source
John J. Wilson, *Tales of the Borders*, vol. 4, p. 159

7   A Convent and a Meeting of Poets

The poets Burns and Scott did not meet in a convent parlour. It is indeed difficult to picture the former in such a devout setting, and the latter was not yet the poet he would become. But on the site of the house in the Sciennes district of Edinburgh in which they met for the only time in their respective lives, the chapel of the convent of St Catherine of Siena had once stood. Dominican nuns had gathered there for Mass and the recital of Offices.

The chapel was built in 1512 on land given a few years earlier by Sir John Crauford, prebendary of St Giles, a devout priest who offered his gift 'To the glory of Almighty God, to the glorious Virgin Mary His Mother undefiled, to St John the Baptist and to St John the Evangelist and all the Saints of Paradise.'

A chaplain was to be appointed who every day 'shall be ready at the high altar to celebrate Mass . . . every Monday a Mass of Requiem and every Friday of the wounds of Our Lord Jesus Christ.' He must not be absent without leave for more than fifteen consecutive days. 'Nor shall it be lawful for the said chaplain to keep a loose woman or concubine in his chamber at home, nor to play cards nor to be a common gamester or engage in similar games of chance.'

Besides the chaplain there was to be a hermit to serve him, 'a man of advanced age, of good life, and of sound constitution' (a practical qualification: a feeble old man, however godly, would be of small help). This server 'shall always live at the same church and shall be his hermit, and is bound to continual residence and the offering of daily prayers for the souls of departed benefactors'. The hermit must 'clean and purify the said church from all dirt and shall serve the priest who is celebrating with water, fire and salt, and shall attend on the celebration of masses' – an excellent balance of duty and devotion, work and prayer.

Sir John himself was the first priest – for four years. Then some devout ladies of high rank implored the establishment of a convent of Dominican nuns. The good Sir John gave them all they desired. Besides his chapel he made over to them land for the building of a convent.

The Dominican friars were a preaching order. The nuns were enclosed, dedicated to a life of prayer and contemplation. They also decided to open a school for girls of good families. The foundation was laid, the building begun and completed, the convent opened and dedicated to St Catherine of Siena, who had been a tertiary of the Dominican Order, living her life of intense and exalted devotion at home.

The sisters arrived; their first prioress, Josine Henryson, was elected and to 'the laif of the Sisters of that ordour of Saint Katerine of Senis' the land and buildings were transferred. Thus the saint's birthplace is on the way to being spelled 'Sciennes.'

A further gift of land was made by a generous layman, John Cant, who owned the grange of St Giles; today there is Grange Road to remind us.

Those devout ladies had their desire, soon and in good measure, with the papal blessing of Leo X, 'servant of the servants of God' to use that noblest of titles.

The convent had a brief but golden day of life. The avalanche of the Reformation soon descended, sweeping away convents and monasteries, nuns, monks and Mass priests, making the Mass illegal. In 1560 the Reformed Church was established in Scotland.

The last prioress was Christian Bellenden, kinswoman of Sir John Bellenden, Justice Clerk. The sub-prioresses included Elizabeth Napier, Elizabeth Auchinleck, widow of Sir William Douglas who was slain at Flodden, one Jacinta whose surname is not recorded, other three ladies Napier and Lady (Jane) Seton, daughter of the first Earl of Bothwell and widow of the third Earl of Seton, also slain at Flodden. When she died in 1558, her successor as sub-prioress was Katherine Seton, daughter of George, second Earl of Seton. She died in 1559, and so came the end of an old and holy song.

Convent and chapel crumbled. No black-robed, veiled figures moved serenely about; there was no longer 'the blessed mutter of the Mass.' Only the name remained, and still remains, in St Catherine's Place.

St Mary's Wynd from the Pleasance

The district became one of comely houses, and on the site
of the chapel, two hundred years later, stood Sciennes Hill
House. In 1786 it belonged to that excellent scholar Adam
Ferguson, Professor of Moral Philosophy in the University of
Edinburgh.

One evening that winter Ferguson had a party of guests, some
of great distinction. The guest of honour was the poet Robert
Burns, then at the height of his fame and favour. There were
some young guests too, among them Walter Scott, the future
poet, then a schoolboy of fifteen, come over from his home in
George Square; he was the son of the worthy lawyer Mr Scott,
grandson of the distinguished physician Dr Rutherford; a nice
lad himself, though of no notable intellectual brilliance in class –
said, however, by his schoolmates to be a great hand at the
telling of old tales. Years later Scott wrote an account of it to his
son-in-law (and biographer) J. G. Lockhart:

> Of course we youngsters sat silent, looked and listened. The
> only thing I remember which was remarkable in Burn's
> manner was the effect produced on him by a print of
> Bunbury's representing a soldier lying dead on the snow,
> his dog sitting by in misery on the one side, on the other his
> widow with a child in her arms. These lines were written
> beneath:
>
> > 'Cold on Canadian hills or Minden's plain
> > Perhaps that parent wept her soldier slain
> > Bent o'er her babe her eyes dissolved in dew
> > The big drops mingling with the milk he drew,
> > Gave the sad presage of his future years,
> > The child of misery baptised in tears.'
>
> Burns seemed much affected by the print, or rather by the
> ideas it suggested to his mind. He actually shed tears. He asked
> whose lines they were, and it chanced that nobody but myself
> remembered that they occur in a half-forgotten poem of
> Longborne called by the unpromising title of 'The Justice of
> the Peace'. I whispered my information to a friend present
> who mentioned it to Burns, who rewarded me with a look and
> a word which though of mere civility, I then received and still
> recollect with very great pleasure.

But to a shy boy a look and word may be unforgettable, unforgotten.

Ten years later, in 1796, Burns was dead, leaving his rich legacy of song and poetry; Walter Scott, the young advocate, beginning to collect ballads and unearth traditions of old buildings, was deeply in love with Williamina Belsches, who, though liking him very well, would not return that love and left a wound in his heart that did not heal. For solace and catharsis he wrote some poems, though not his best.

Later came Scott's full power and inspiration. In some of his poems, notably 'The Lay of the Last Minstrel,' and in his novels of medieval and earlier Europe he brought back something of the ethos and ambience of the old religion. His innumerable admirers, whatever their creed, became aware of a heritage they had not known existed.

In 1833, the year after Scott's death, the Oxford or Tractarian Movement revived, in the Church of England, still more of her heritage in doctrine and liturgy. Later some of the Tractarians transferred their allegiance to Rome, notably among them Newman and Manning.

Along with Henry Manning, the future Cardinal, came his friend James Hope-Scott, husband of Charlotte Lockhart, Scott's only descendant and heiress. There was now a chapel at Abbotsford where Mass were celebrated, and once Newman came to stay. The Real Presence in the Reserved Sacrament is at the heart of Scott's home today.

So the Wizard of the North was permitted, perhaps unconsciously inspired, to work a holy spell. His benign presence is still about the house. Perhaps St Catherine and her holy priests and nuns were not driven utterly out of Scotland. There may have been a presence, a holy haunting, about that house of Sciennes where two poets met in mutual courtesy.

Source
Sir Walter Scott in J. G. Lockhart, *Life of Scott*, vol. 1, pp. 150–5

8   Mirror, Mirror on the Wall

Lady Stair, who gave her name to the close off Edinburgh's High Street, was, in her middle and later years, a very great lady, secure in rank and in estimation. But in her youth, at the end of the seventeenth century, she had come very near to a tragic end. As a girl she was married off to Lord Primrose, one of the city's most notorious profligates, a young man completely devoid of morals. In cruelty and depravity he surpassed most rivals. They were hardly ever together. His family made some effort of reconciliation but that was impossible.

One morning, as Lady Primrose was in her room, dressing, she saw in the mirror the door open, slowly, stealthily; her husband came slinking in, carrying a drawn sword. He did not realize that she could see his reflection, as he came sliding over the floor. The brave lass jumped out of the open window and, half-dressed though she was, ran to the house of her mother-in-law, where she demanded and received shelter and protection. There was no more talk of a reconciliation.

Soon after that, Lord Primrose went abroad. No one tried to follow him or to discover his whereabouts. Life went on. Lady Primrose had good friends, and she lived quietly and discreetly but not withdrawn from society.

About that time there was a great deal of talk about a conjuror and fortune-teller who had taken lodgings in the Canongate. He was said to have a marvellous gift of second sight. If told about some absent member of a family, given even a slight clue he could give an account which later proved true. He was very much in demand and often consulted.

Lady Primrose decided to go to him. She persuaded a friend to accompany her. They went wearing homely clothes, wrapped in a maidservant's cloak with a plaid hood. They were received with grave and discreet courtesy, no names given or asked. Lady Primrose described her husband. Could the magician – as indeed the man appeared to be – give any account of him?

'Come here. Look in the mirror on the wall.' She looked into a

Regent Murray's house in the Canongate

large mirror. There was no reflection of herself, of the seer or of the room where they sat. A swirling of mist dissolved, a picture appeared, very clearly. The scene was a large church, with a group of people gathered together; at the chancel steps facing the clergyman stood a bridal pair. The bridegroom turned his head to look at the bride, and Lady Primrose recognized clearly and beyond doubt – her husband.

There was a shout, a rush of feet and a young man ran in, carrying a sword. He rushed towards the bridegroom, there was much shouting and confusion, then the scene dissolved into mist, but not before Lady Primrose had recognized the intruder. He was her brother whom she knew to be abroad at the time.

The vision was a shock but, except for its vehicle, no surprise. The lady was very composed. She thanked the seer, paid him his fee and walked silently home with her companion, who was also discreetly silent. She had seen no vision in the mirror but she asked no questions.

As soon as she was in her own room again, Lady Primrose sat down at her desk to write a full account of what she had seen. Then, calling a witness, she signed and sealed the paper and put it into a drawer and locked the drawer, giving the key to the witness.

Not long afterwards her brother came home and at once visited her. He asked whether she had had any news of her husband, then told her his own account of what she had seen reflected in the mirror.

While he was in Holland, in Rotterdam, he had met and done some business with a wealthy merchant who was a much respected citizen. They had become friendly, and one day the merchant had told him that his daughter was to be married the very next day to a Scot. His fellow Scot must come to the marriage. It was all very courteous and cordial. The brother was delayed by some business, went hastily to the church and from the doorway recognized his brother-in-law. Then he had rushed in, shouting, 'Stop, I forbid the banns. This man is already married,' and the scene of confusion had followed. The evil bridegroom had fled and none pursued him.

Lady Primrose listened quietly. Then she sent for the witness and asked for the key to the drawer. Without a word she opened it and handed her brother the paper with the account of all she had seen in the mirror on the wall.

The fugitive never returned. Not long afterwards news came of his death. He was not greatly mourned.

Her second marriage, to Lord Stair, was happier but not entirely tranquil. He was a devoted husband but was too often roarin fou*, coming home completely out of control of his actions. One night he attacked her so violently as to draw blood from her face, he then fell into a drunken slumber. His wife, already trained in marital violence, did nothing. She did not wash the blood from her face but sat beside her husband, weeping. When he awoke, sober and clear in mind and sight, he looked with amazed horror at her face, soaked in tear and blood.

'Whit ails ye?' he asked her. She told him of his actions.

In horror and remorse he vowed that he would never again accept drink but from her hands, and he kept his vow. He went no more to convivialities in other company, in taverns or the homes of cronies. The Stairs gave excellent parties, at which her ladyship sat beside his lordship and handed him his wine, in what she thought was a discreet amount. This he accepted gratefully. When she withdrew, she left one glass and, having drunk that, he drank no more. The marriage became and continued to be happy.

Lady Stair survived her husband by twelve years to see and doubtless enjoy that major drama the *Douglas Cause*, which concerned the succession to the dukedom of Douglas. The Duke was childless and refused to acknowledge as heirs the twin boys born to his sister Lady Jane at the age of fifty after a secret marriage. Lady Stair was friendly with the Duke and Duchess and was acutely embarrassed to hear that the Earl of Dundonald had told the Duke that Lady Stair did not believe the twins were truly the sons of Lady Jane Stewart and her husband. Therefore neither they nor Lady Jane had any claim on the Duke. Dundonald had further enraged her by writing a letter to the Lord Justice Clerk, repeating this statement and adding that he would let anyone and everyone call him a damned villain if he did not speak the truth.

Her ladyship was neither to haud nor to bind.* She descended upon the Duke and Duchess in their apartments in Holyrood, stamped into the room, stood leaning on her staff and declared that the Earl of Dundonald was indeed a damned villain. Having spoken, she stamped her staff three times on the floor. She was now, she told them, of a great age, but never until now had she been involved in clatters* or scandal.

Perhaps one may question that. There was a tale or legend about her marriage that, with the memories of her first disastrous union with Lord Primrose, she had been reluctant to accept this second wooer; that he had lost patience, entered her house one evening, unknown to her, and bribed her servant to let him hide in a small ante-room where Lady Primrose used to come every morning to say her prayers. He stood at the window, at an early hour, undressed; the marriage followed soon after.

Lady Stair lived until 1759. More than two centuries later a postscript was added by that distinguished woman of letters Rosaline Masson, daughter of Professor David Masson. She discovered in the marriage register of a London church, St Peter's upon Cornhill, the certificate of marriage between Lord Stair and Lady Primrose, March 1702, some years before the date of that scandalous appearance. With an acute sense of

Cowgate looking east

justice and of irony, Miss Masson sent her account of the discovery to *Chambers' Journal*.

Sources
Robert Chambers, *Traditions of Edinburgh*
The story (giving the characters different names) is also told by Scott in *My Aunt Margaret's Mirror*

9 The Unsanctified

Edinburgh is near enough to the Borders to share the legendary of witchcraft. The High Court of Justiciary heard many cases.

There were, beyond doubt, many unjust condemnations. Old women living alone, grown malignant from neighbourly un-kindness, were most often suspect. They were often accused and often executed.

It was not only the obscure who faced this most dreadful charge. One of the most distinguished citizens and officials in the city was the Lord Lyon King at Arms, Sir William Stewart, who in August 1568 was 'transported from Edinburgh Castel to Dunbrittan [Dumbarton] and there committed to close prisone for conspyring to take the Regent's lyfe by sorcery and necromancy, for which he was put to Death.'

Another version of this is given in a letter from Lord Hunsdon to Sir William Cecil: 'Steward who was King of Heralds . . . had determined to kill the Regent; but he was forgiven for that, and was brunt for Conjuration and Witchcraft.'

There is a touch of black humour about this: the conspiracy itself was not a capital charge; it was to be 'forgiven' – almost with the admonition not to do it again, but the sorcery and conjuration of devils, for whatever purpose, brought condemnation.

The Regent was that other Stewart, the Earl of Moray, half-brother of Queen Mary. An Act of 1563 decreed that: 'Nae person take upon hand to use ony manner of witchcraft, sorcery or necromancy, nor give themselves furth to have ony sic craft or knowledge thereof, there-through abusing the people . . .' and 'that nae person seek ony help response or consultation at ony sic users or abusers of witchcraft . . . under the pain of death'.

James VI had an obsession about witches and witchcraft – perhaps having heard of the strange case that occurred at the time of his birth in Edinburgh Castle, when, in another room in the castle, the Countess of Atholl was giving birth to a child, and she was believed to have magical powers.

One Andrew Lundie told John Knox five years later that he had come to the castle on some business and asked for the wet-nurse, Lady Reres, 'whom he fand in her chalmer, lying bedfast, and he asking of her disease she answerit that she was never so troubled with no bairn that ever she bare, for the Lady Athole had casten all the pyne of her childbirth upon her . . .'

Robert Chambers, who quoted this account, added that the pain of childbirth could be cast not only upon another woman but on a man or on an animal. Some years later an enchantress of the upper ranks called Euphan McCalyean while in childbed had a bored stone laid under her pillow, a magic powder rolled up in her hair and, as the charge against her stated: 'her guid man's sark* taen aff him and laid womplit* under your bed feet; the whilk being pratisit, your sickness was casten aff you unnaturally, upon an dog, whilk ran away and was never seen again.'

Suspected witches were tried before the High Court of Justiciary, and witnesses were summoned who deponed* against the accused. If they were found guilty, as was usually the case, they were burned at the stake. The trial in the High Court was usually preceded by one before the kirk session or the local presbytery, whose findings were given serious hearing. The kirk had great power, as intense, if not as wide, as that of the hated Papacy. Indeed, the closest parallel to those witch trials was probably the Spanish Inquisition.

Robert Pitcairn, in his long record of criminal trials, recounts more than one of witchcraft, sorcery and necromancy, including that of Janet Boyman, spouse to William Steil,

> Delated of diverse crimes of witchcraft.
> Convict and brint.

Such trials continued beyond the reign of James VI. In 1629 Alexander Hamilton, 'a notorious warlock', was imprisoned in the Tolbooth. He informed on some women, especially Katharine Oswald of Niddry, said to have insensitivity to pain, a characteristic of witches. One of the tests was pricking with a pin: this would be felt by an honest woman but not by a witch. Witnesses had seen 'ane preen put into the heid by John Aird, minister, in the panel's shoulder being the devil's mark, and nae bluid following nor she naeways shrinking thereat.'

Hamilton had been with Katharine at witches' covens between Niddry and Edmonston where they met the Devil. She had been at another coven at Prestonpans in March 1625, 'the night of the great storm.' This poor woman was convicted and burned. Yet she had cast no evil spells; indeed she had performed cures.

Hamilton himself was tried in January 1630. It was stated or deponed that he had met the Devil, in the form of a black man, on Kingston Hill near Haddington. He had been told how to raise him by striking three times on the ground with a stick of fir, and calling, 'Rise up, foul thief.' Sometimes he summoned the Devil in form of a dog or a crow.

Hamilton was malignant. He burned a grain mill, not by direct arson but by burning three stalks of corn with appropriate intention and incantation. He was tried before the Privy Council, convicted and burned.

Alice Nisbet had worked both good and ill. She had cured a woman by bathing her feet and legs in hot water into which she had dipped her own fingers: the magic touch. Then she had run widdershins* round the bed crying, 'The bones to the fire and the soul to the Devil.' Finally she had put that woman's sickness upon another woman, who had died within twenty-four hours.

One of the most famous – or infamous – and most pitiful cases is that of Bessie Dunlop, in November 1576. Whether she was under delusion or whether she truly had knowledge and skill beyond that of ordinary mortals is uncertain. What is certain is that she did no evil and much good, working cures through herbs and finding lost possessions. If she was a witch, it was a white and beneficent magic she worked.

Bessie was the wife of a farmer, Andrew Jack, in Ayrshire. Her tale has been told in Robert Pitcairn's *Criminal Trials*, with all the 'facts' or confessions extorted from her by prosecution, by witnesses, before the Church courts and finally the Justiciary.

Pitcairn called this 'one of the earliest and may assuredly be reckoned as one of the most extraordinary cases on record, in reference to the infatuation, common to all nations of Europe at that period on the subject of witchcraft.' It is also one of the most cruel, most indefensible. Pitcairn finds it – as does the modern reader – particularly interesting, for '. . . the very minute and yet graphic details given by Bessie of many circumstances connected with the prevailing superstition, especially in relation to the Court of Fairye . . . Few scenes perhaps are anywhere to be met with so intensely attractive as the meetings with Thom Reid.' (He, it may be noted, has the same Christian name as Thomas the Rhymer and Tam Linn, both of whom dwelt long in the Court of faery, but there was a real Thom Reid, 'an officiare to the Lard of Blair'.)

Pitcairn tries to make rational diagnosis of Bessie's case: hallucination. She was probably 'the dupe of her own over-heated imagination, already well stored with such fancies before her first interview with Thom Reid, who, if not entirely the phantom of a disordered brain, may not unlikely have been some heartless wag acquainted with the virtues and the use of herbs, and may have played off this too fatal joke.' We are not quite rational, perhaps; today we are more aware of the borderlines of the mind.

If the above theory of Thom is sound, then 'wag' is too good a word to use of him. If he were merely and entirely human, he was possessed by diabolic ingenuity, and he brought to destruction this poor innocent – for that was what she was, in both senses of the word: guiltless and lacking common worldly sense. Bessie may be best seen as a holy fool, of which there are many in legend. But the holy fool may win when the worldly wise fail. Bessie, poor woman, had no such triumph.

These trials of witches, first before kirk session and presbytery and then in the High Court, brought many witnesses and many statements and admissions from the panel or accused. Confession was elicited by fiendish tortures. The mildest of these were solitary confinement, abandonment by kinsfolk, depriva-tion of food, drink and sleep, until at last the poor women, 'weary of life', made confessions. Torture was used also in the name of religion, by Catholics against heretics, by Protestants against Catholics. In our own century many of those subtleties were re-discovered and used by Hitler and his fellow fiends.

Trial and condemnation of witches was, as Pitcairn found, as often 'for abusing [deluding] the people with their "devilitch craft" as for the act of witchcraft', and there was plenty of opportunity for malicious neighbours to make accusations.

One of the worst tortures was that of the witches' bridle, an instrument rarely equalled in the annals of torment: 'By means of a hoop passed over the head, a piece of iron having four points or prongs, was forcibly thrust into the mouth two of these being directed to the tongue and cheek, the others pointing outwards to each cheek. The infernal machine was secured by a padlock.' The victim was 'waked' by some 'skilful person' – skilful, that is, at keeping prisoners awake. A few days of this torture made the poor creature willing to make any confession. There were many examinations; the clergy and elders of the kirk were willing interrogators. Then came the formal trial.

The confessions were read; the prisoner in the dock was further interrogated; there might be witnesses; doom was pronounced, and within a few days the victim could be led to the stake to be 'strangled and burnt to ashes.'

At her trial, Elizabeth or Bessie Dunlop, asked how she cured the sick, told people where to find lost or stolen property – 'things that tyn or were stollen away', replied that she consulted Thom Reid, who told her whatever she asked. What kind of man was he? A good and honest man, grey-haired, dressed in a grey coat and breeches, white 'shanks' (stockings) gartered above the knee. He wore a black bonnet and carried a white wand. How and where did he first come to her? When she was leading her cows to pasture, crying in distress for a cow that had died and for her husband and their child who were grievously sick.

He had greeted her: 'Gude day to ye, Bessie', and she had replied, 'Gude [God] speed ye, gude man' – a pious greeting from one who, if a witch, would dread the Holy Name. Then he had asked, also with a holy exclamation, '*Sancta Maria*, why make you such dule and sair greeting – for ony warldlie thing?' (Our Lady's name was still spoken by devout Catholics, rarely by Protestants, and not by witches or warlocks or any of the 'Other People.')

'Our gear is brakit [damaged or lost], my husband at the point of death, my babe will not live. Have I not cause to weep?' It is a poignant cry, with the ring of a ballad.

Thom was very stern, almost pitiless, telling her that she had 'effendit and crabit God', asking Him for something she should not have. Her child must die, a sheep would die as well as the cow, but her husband would recover and be 'as hale and fair as ever he was.' She must ask pardon of God and make amends.

'And then I was somewhat blyther for he told me my gude man would mend.'

Thom left her and went away; his departure was somewhat uncanny. 'I thocht he gaed in at ane narrower hole in the dyke than onie earthly man could hae gone through, and I was something fleyed and feart.'

Another meeting was by a thorn tree near her house. (The thorn had a magic significance.) He tarried a while with her. Would she not trow (trust) in him? She had answered that she would trust in anyone who did her good. Then he promised her 'much gear', cattle and horses if she would renounce her baptismal vows and deny her Christian faith. This she declared she would never do, even if she were to be torn apart by horses. This angered him and he left her.

His next appearance was in her own house, her husband and others being present. Taking hold of her by her apron, he led her to the door and outside, with none following. There he forbade

The Levee Room in Regent Murray's house with the remarkable thorn planted by Queen Mary

her to speak of anything she might see or hear. Then she saw twelve persons, four men and eight women, the men 'in gentlemen's clothes, the women wrapped in plaids all very comely like to see'.

Interrogated (had she known any of them?), she answered, 'None but Thom.' Had they spoken to her and what had they said? They had bade her sit down and had said, 'Welcome Bessie, wilt thou go with us?' But she 'had answered nocht' because Thom had forbidden her to speak. 'Within a short space they pairtit all awa.' Then 'ane hideous uglie sowch [sough, blast of wind]' followed them, and she 'lay sick' until Thom 'came back fra them.' They had spoken together; she had seen their lips move but could hear nothing. Interrogated whether she had 'speired at him who these persons were', she answered that they were 'the good wights who dwelt in the Court of Elfhame' who had come to invite her to go with them. But she had refused, 'seeing nae profit in it, and would not go without good reason'. Thom had tried to lure her, offering a subtle and clever temptation.

'See thou nocht me baith meat-worth and claith-worth and gude eneugh like in person?' – well-fed, well-clad, comely and healthy. He could 'make her far better nor ever she was.' To this the good woman replied that she 'dwelt with her ain husband and bairns and could not leave them.' This made Thom 'verrie crabit' and angry, and he told her she would now 'get little good of him.'

She was interrogated further: had she asked any favours of Thom? She answered, yes, when a neighbour came to consult her about sick animals, a cow or a ewe or one 'elf-grippit', Thom would pull a herb, bid her mix it with other herbs, seethe and strain it and make a liquor or salve, or dry the herbs to a powder. Put it into the animal's mouth 'and the beast would mend.' There were herbs too that, as drink or salve, would heal sickness and pain in people. They too would mend. She had given such healing medicines and salves to sick children and those in pain, and they would recover – if they did not sweat. But a patient who did not absorb the salve, who sweated it out, would die.

Three times Thom had given her the healing herbs with his own hand. He had told her what to do, how to make a medicine or a salve.

To whom had she given such medicine? The Lady Johnstone had sent to her begging her 'to help ane young gentill-woman, her dochter now mairit on the young Laird o' Stonelie.' Bessie had gone to Thom, who had diagnosed the sickness as 'a cauld blude that gaed aboot hir hart and causit hir to dwam and vigour away [to faint].' Bessie was to seethe (boil) ginger, cloves, aniseed and liquorice in stark (strong) ale, syphon it and give it to the patient to drink in the morning and some hours later, before dinner. The lady recovered. (It sounds an excellent tonic in health as well as in sickness.) Where had Bessie seen her patient and given her the drink? In the house of her sister-in-law, Lady Blackhall. Had Bessie been given any payment? Yes, a sack of meal and some cheese.

Had anyone else consulted her? Yes, the old Lady Kilbowie, about her crooked leg. Bessie had gone to Thom, who had told her there was no cure, for the cause was that the marrow was 'consumit' and the blood lost. If the old lady sought further help, 'it wad be waur for hir.' (A good doctor knows when a case is incurable.)

Had she gone to any women in childbirth? Only after consulting Thom. Once he had given her a silk lace or tie which he told her to bind round the woman's arm. She did so, and the woman had a quick and good delivery. Once Thom had come to Bessie herself when she was in labour, assuring her that all would be well, and so it was.

Could she forsee and foretell anything that was to come? Nothing of herself; only if Thom told her. She could do nothing without him.

Many came to ask her to find stolen goods. One lady had lost 'two hornes of gold and ane crown of the same', and Bessie had told her where they were. She had recovered clothes and barley stolen from a barn, but once she failed. A stolen cloak could not be recovered because it had been made into a kirtle. (There is a realism in those findings and a touch of the comic. The kirtle could not be proved to have been a cloak.)

At what time did Thom usually appear to her? 'The twelfth hour of the day was his common appearing.' She was forbidden to speak to him until he spoke to her. Once, when she was in childbed, a stout woman appeared and sat by her and asked for food and drink, which she was given. She then told Bessie that her child would die but that her husband would live. This, said Thom, was his mistress, the Queen of Elfhame.

Had she ever seen Thom by the waterside? Once at Leith, where she had gone with her husband; once at Restalrig Loch, where she saw a company of riders that 'made sic a dyn as heavin and erd had gane togidder, and incontinent thai raid into the loch with many hideous rumbill.'

When did she last see Thom? The day after Candlemas, when he told her of bad weather to come. (Maybe she recalled the weather rhyme:

> If Candlemas be clear and fair
> The hauf o the winter's tae come and mair;
> If Candlemas be dull and foul,
> The hauf o the winter's by at Yule.)

Had Thom ever warned her of her fate as a witch? He had foretold trouble but had bidden her go to neighbours for protection, and the Bishop of Glasgow would help her.

Finally verdict was given.

New Town from the north west

The said Elizabeth Dunlop being on pannell accused by the
Dittay [indictment] openly read in judgement . . . re-enterit
again to the said Court of Justiciary and thair in the presence
of the Lord Justice Depute by thair deliverance pronouncit
and deliverit by the mouth and speiking of Andro Crauford,
the said Elizabeth Dunlop to be culpable, fylit and convict in
haill points above written of using Witch craft, Sorcerie and
Incantatioun and Incantatioun of the Devill, continuand in
familaritie with thame at all times as she thocht expedient, and
thereby dealing with charms, and abusing the people with her
devilish craft of sorcerie.

Bessie was 'convict and brynt.' Her poor body in ashes, her soul
went to a judge more merciful than any upon earth.

Source
Robert Pitcarin, *Ancient Criminal Trials in Scotland*

10 Gabriel's Road

Edinburgh has the duality of good and evil, of culture and crime, in her streets and lanes and in her very bones. One of the most horrible murders in the history of crime was committed in 1717 in what is now the New Town, in a road which later held that genial resort of men of letters Ambrose's Tavern.

The story is told laconically by Robert Chambers in his *Traditions of Edinburgh*, more vividly by J. G. Lockhart, who wrote when a young man under the name of Dr Peter Morris, a middle-aged Welshman visiting Edinburgh, making many friendships and reporting in *Peter's Letters to his Kinsfolk*. Lockhart introduces his other self to his friends and to their meeting-places, of which one of the most delightful is Ambrose's Tavern.

Dr Morris was happy to be invited to this famous inn, where he enjoyed an excellent dinner, the main course being Tay salmon, and drank thereafter a noble port. He heard the name of the small road, almost lane, where it stood, Gabriel's Road, and he heard the source of the name and the story of the murder, which he found 'one of the most striking illustrations I have ever met with of the effects of puritanical superstition in destroying the moral feelings.'

Gabriel was a young man, a 'licentiate' in the Church of Scotland – licensed to preach but not yet ordained to the full ministry or qualified for a parish. Like many such, he had a tutor's post in a gentleman's house, teaching the two small sons, aged ten and eight.

The lady of the house had a very pretty maid, and the tutor looked upon her with admiration and desire. He did no more, however, than kiss her one day, passing through the room where she sat with her needlework. But his elder pupil saw him, thought this an immense joke and told his brother. Together they took the joke to their mother, who thought it neither funny nor proper, although she was not gravely scandalized. She did, however, utter a word or reproof to the tutor which he took very

East side of St Andrew's Square

badly. A sense of guilt, of resentment that these boys should make fun of him, that his name should be darkened, worked in his mind and rose to a fury.

On the following Sabbath Gabriel took his pupils to church and afterwards for a walk in the fields just beyond the town, in what soon became the New Town, just over the gulf which was to be bridged and lead to Princes Street, to Register House and to Ambrose's Tavern. There in the fields he stabbed the elder boy in the heart, splashing the knife and his own evil hand with the child's blood. The younger boy stood for a moment, then fled, but he was overtaken and stabbed in his turn, and innocent blood flowed again.

Incredibly all this was done in full daylight and within sight of many citizens walking in the Old Town. They could not save the boys but they could and did seize their murderer.

They brought Gabriel to the magistrates who were assembled in the City Chambers ready to walk in solemn procession to the kirk of St Giles. The murderer's hands were still red with the blood of his victims, and he still held the knife within their bloody grasp. He had been caught literally red-handed.

It is an old law in Scotland that the murderer thus caught need not be brought to trial but may be executed forthwith. The crowd dragged Gabriel to justice. He was hanged without trial and without delay. Chambers adds the gruesome detail that his murderous hands were hacked off with the bloodied knife, which then hung round his neck.

Sources
Robert Chambers, *Traditions of Edinburgh* (Chambers rejects the name of Gabriel and gives the murderer's real name as Robert Irvine.)
J. G. Lockhart, *Peter's Letters to his Kinsfolk*

11   A Murder Foiled

The theme of dual personality is recurrent in Scottish literature. The duality may be between some degree of good – at least of respectability, and downright evil, as in *Jekyll and Hyde* and in Hogg's *Confessions of a Justified Sinner*. There is also a duality between sense and a simplicity bordering on the half-wit.

The half-wit has usually been accepted with tolerance, often indulgence, and the belief is common that he is not as daft as he looks, or not daft all the time or altogether. That was probably the neighbours' opinion of Geordie Willison, and a certain great lady must have wished bitterly that he had not so much sense, awareness and tenacity.

George was the son of one Willie Willison who lived in Leith in the eighteenth century. He was a water-carrier, a decent poor man who went round the well-to-do houses with a water-cart drawn by a donkey, earning enough to keep his wife, son and daughter and himself. He was often given a supply of food to take home, an old coat, shoes and the like, so he did none too badly. His one weakness was whisky, *uisge beatha*, the water of life. The water he carried in his cart was a wersh drink.* It was all very well for the gentry who liked to wash in it and have their clothes washed and their floors scrubbed, and who used it for making tea, that genteel drink, but Willie liked his whisky, and whisky and water proved fatal. He did not drink them mixed: he drank his whisky neat. When one day he had drunk more than a dram or two, he fell off his water-cart and it went over him.

Willie was mourned decently but not with great anguish by his widow, a capable woman who managed very well, finding work in some of the houses where her husband had been known; her daughter Kate was like her, a bonny lass who was handy with a needle. As for her son Geordie, some said he'd be no help at all, for he was simple in the mind, just a 'natural', but others declared, 'Bide a bit an see. He's no sae saft* as ye think.' And they were right.

Geordie did not care to stay with one job, but he contrived to

Vegetable and fish market

find some kind of a job every day, as one of the caddies* who hung about the streets, ready to go an errand, carry luggage, fetch a cab or a sedan chair, take letters – anything to be done at short notice. He was not given much money, but there was always something to take home, and he was often given food.

One of his occasional employers was Sir Marmaduke Maitland of Castle Gower in the Borders, a baronet of excellent standing, well known and respected. His property was strictly entailed – it must pass from father to son, or, failing a son, to a daughter, failing both to the next of kin, who must continue the name and style of Maitland of Castle Gower. Sir Marmaduke was married to a kinswoman of Lord Herries in Kirkcudbright, Catherine Maxwell, who thought very well of herself, living in considerable style with a French cook and French housekeeper. Her husband let her have her own way, and he had his. The marriage appeared to hold, if not happily, but the lady brought her husband no heir.

The rich house and the humble one were to be linked by a strange chance (mischance for Lady Maitland, luck for Geordie and the succession).

When Geordie came home one evening, his mother asked him if he had found a job.

'Och aye, I wis helpin Sir Marmaduke Maitland on his wey tae France. I carried his luggage doon tae the ship at Leith, and he gi'ed me this.' He turned out his pockets to reveal some coppers – not a great deal but enough to please his thrifty mother.

'Weel, it's yer birthday the day, Geordie, so we'll e'en hae supper an some ale tae drink yer health.'

As they drank their ale, Geordie's mother asked, 'Is her leddyship awa wi Sir Marmaduke?'

'Na, na. She's bidin at hame, an he'll be gled tae be awa frae her. He disna like her, an it's nae wunner – Ah dinna like her masel.'

'Whit wey no, Geordie?'

'Because she disna like me!' Geordie did not go back to the Maitland mansion.

This was in April, and during the following February he happened to be near that place, having been sent with a letter to the laird of Warriston. It was a pleasant region of fields with trees and hedges, and he walked leisurely along. He met no one, but as he was passing a tall hedge he heard a voice he knew – two voices, in fact: one was that of Lady Maitland, the other of Louise, her French housekeeper. Lady Maitland spoke in her high, imperious tone. Geordie stood listening.

'I cannot do this thing, Louise, though it must be done. The child must not live until Sir Marmaduke comes home. But I am its mother and I cannot do this. You must do it. You shall have ten golden pieces, as I promised.'

'Very good, my lady. I will do it, though I do not like it at all. It will be very easy, she is so small a creature, so new and so feeble.'

'I shall withdraw out of sight but within hearing. Call out when you have done.' There was a rustle of silk skirts, then silence, then a muttering, '*Tiens, tiens*, it is not weak, it is strong, this brat, someone will hear. I must press harder.' Geordie stood frozen with horror. 'There, is it done? No, still the creature breathes. I cannot press harder.'

Lady Maitland called, 'Is it done, Louise?'

'My lady I cannot do it, she is too strong, this infant, she struggles, she will cry. Let me have your hair necklace, that will do the work.'

'I cannot come to you, you must come to me.' Geordie heard Louise run, heard her come back, heard her mutter: 'Ah this will do the work, it is a strong necklace. Lie still, little monster, ah, now I have you – so.'

Then there was silence, except for running footsteps as the woman went back to her mistress. Geordie waited, giving them time to depart. He knew they would not linger. Then he went behind the high hedge and saw, on the ground, a pitifully small object – a baby strangled with the strong hair necklace tight round its tiny throat. Geordie dropped on his knees. He un-wound the cruel string, he blew with all his breath into the child's mouth, and presently he heard a little sigh, the merest flutter of breath – but there *was* breath, and it grew stronger and the child opened its eyes. Geordie picked it up very gently, carried it under his coat and went home.

'Whaur hae ye been, Geordie, an whit's that ye're cairryin?'

'I hae been oot wi a letter and I've been paid for it. An luik, here's a bonny wee birdie I fund and hae brocht tae ye.'

At first his mother was too astonished to speak. She took the tiny baby from him and, looking at the pitifully swollen little face and at the mark on her neck, came near to tears.

'Puir wee lambie, puir wee birdie. Hush ye noo. But wha is this bairn, Geordie? Whaur did ye find it? Whit ah'm ah tae dae wi it?'

'Ye ken better whit tae dae wi a bairn than ah dae. Ye didna speir whaur I cam frae when ye had me, an Ah'm no tellin ye ony mair. Gie the wee bit thing some milk.'

His mother obeyed both her son and her own motherly instincts. She asked no more and warned Kate to be silent too. They knew Geordie's dour temper. He was placid and easy most of the time, but his obstinacy was hard as a stone, and if plagued with questions he could become fierce. So the good woman took charge of the baby, fed her with drops of milk, wrapped her in a warm shawl and put her to bed. While she was busy, Geordie picked up the clothes she had taken off the child, and locked them into his own chest, along with the hair necklace. Nothing more was said.

The neighbours were somehow given to understand that the child was Mrs Willison's grand-daughter, the child of an older daughter who lived in the country and who had died in child-birth. It could have been that, or the child could have been Geordie's – though people doubted that; anyway there were no questions, and the baby was well cherished.

One question his mother asked: 'Wha's tae pey fir the bairn's keep?' Geordie replied. 'Masel. Ye'll no lack ony money. Never fear on that score.'

Next day Geordie went out to the Maitland mansion. He asked at the back door very politely. 'Wull ye take me to her leddyship? I hae an important message fir her.' He was holding a folded paper. He was taken at once to the lady's drawing-room. Geordie was known by the servants, for he had done many an errand for Sir Marmaduke; they might think him a bit wanting but a douce, civil fellow.

'Gude day tae yer leddyship,' said Geordie. The lady stared at him coldly.

'How did you come here? What do you want? Leave this room at once.' She rose and was moving towards the bell to summon a servant.

'Canny noo,* leddy,' said Geordie. 'Ye maunna be sae hasty. But mebbe ye're no recovered frae that cauld wait that ye had oot at Warriston. It canna hae been gude for a delicate leddy like yersel – an you scarce recovered.'

The lady stood still, as if frozen, as if changed into a statue.

'I wadna trouble yer leddyship but I'm in want o siller. I ken ye're leddyship's generosity. Sir Marmaduke wha wad hae helpit me is no here, sae I hae ventured tae come tae yersel.' He stood very respectfully, holding his bonnet in his hand. He looked at her steadily.

'How much do you want?'

'£20, yer leddyship, wad last me for a while an be weel spent. I wadna ask mair, I'll no hae fowk speirin whaur I got the money a o a sudden. Twenty punds will dae me a gude whilie, an if I may luik on yer leddyship as my banker I'll ca on ye again – tho no ower soon.'

The lady moved slowly to her desk, took twenty £1 notes from a drawer and handed them, silently, to Geordie. He counted them carefully and put them with equal care into an inner pocket of his coat. 'I'm obliged tae yer leddyship. Gude day tae ye,' and he went off as quietly as he had come.

He was sure now of what he had suspected: Lady Maitland had had a child by a lover, and she believed the child to be dead. He did not intend to remove that belief. If she knew that the child was alive and in the keeping of Geordie and his mother, she would somehow, with the help of Louise, find the poor little thing and make sure of its being done to death – perhaps even of making it appear that Geordie was guilty. He would not trust her, for he knew her to be a merciless, vindictive woman. Meanwhile, he had her in his power and he had £20 and would have more when he needed it. Yet some thought Geordie saft!

He went home with his £20 in his pocket, and that evening as they sat by the fire he handed one of them to his mother. 'Here, tak that for the bairn's needs. When ye want mair, let me ken.' His mother looked at him astonished, with a question in her eye but none on her lips. She looked at Kate, who also kept silent. 'Thank ye, Geordie,' and that ended the matter.

Life went on much as usual with the Willisons. Geordie found jobs but sometimes did without one if he did not fancy it. Kate found a sweetheart, one Dempster, a decent fellow who had been butler to Sir Marmaduke. He had been dismissed after Sir Marmaduke went abroad, because her ladyship disliked him and preferred a French manservant. But, as he told Kate after they were married, he had heard some gossip and rumour that the false wife had had a lover, to whom she had borne a child, and that the child had never been seen. There were dark mutters but no one dared to speak out or report their suspicions. He asked no questions about the bairn his brother-in-law had brought home, though he may well have discussed the mystery with Kate. It is probable that he had his own ideas. Meanwhile he was in service with Sir Marmaduke's nephew, next-of-kin and heir presumptive, a rakish young man called Ludovic Brodie from whom Sir Marmaduke had little respect or affection. But the law of entail could not be set aside.

Next year Geordie went out again to the Maitland mansion. Sir Marmaduke was still abroad – he had many interests, and he was in no hurry to return to a wife to whom he was no more devoted than she to him. He had a trustworthy man of affairs to look after his estate.

On this visit Geordie met Louise, who from her foreign look he guessed to be the woman whose voice he had heard beyond

Leith harbour from the pier

the hedge. To make sure, he asked her politely, 'Wad ye be sae guid, ma'am, as tae tak me tae her leddyship. I hae a message fir her.'

'What can a fellow like you possibly want with her ladyship? Let me have your message and I shall take it to her. I am her housekeeper, Mademoiselle Louise Grécourt.' It was the voice he remembered.

'Thank ye kindly, ma'am, but Ah maun speak tae her leddyship hersel. Juist tell her that Geordie Willison is here to speak wi her.' The Frenchwoman obeyed. Geordie entered the room.

'I hope yer leddyship is weel. Ye may hae been thinkin I hae forgotten oor meetin juist a year ago – but Ah'm no ane tae forget.'

'What do you want?' asked her ladyship.

'Just £20, as before.' Again he was given silently twenty £1 notes; again he bowed, 'My thanks tae yer leddyship and gude day,' and he went home.

Next year he came again, asked and received the same amount. It was all given, a pound at a time, to his mother, for the child, who was a bonny and healthy bairn, well cared for, cherished by that kindly woman. She had been named Jessie Warriston, her Christian name from Mrs Willison, her surname from the place where Geordie had found and rescued her.

Not long after his third visit to Lady Maitland, Geordie was on the dock at Leith, waiting for a boat to come in, hoping to be taken on by someone as a porter or caddie for his luggage. Among the first to disembark was Sir Marmaduke Maitland, who recognized Geordie and engaged him to carry his bags to his carriage, mount beside the coachman and carry them up to the house. He was one of those who thought Geordie a bit wanting, but amusing, and he enjoyed a gossip with him. So Geordie walked up to the door with Sir Marmaduke, entertaining him with the daft kind of talk expected of him. Lady Maitland and Louise stood at the door, the same fear in both their minds. Was Geordie telling Sir Marmaduke what he knew? But he seemed merely to be talking nonsense.

'An what's new, Geordie?' asked Sir Marmaduke, when he had greeted his wife and walked into his hall. 'Ye'll not have been here, I'm thinking, while I've been away.' He knew his wife's dislike of Geordie. 'I've no been here sae aften as when yersel's at hame, Sir Marmaduke. But her leddyship has been sae kind as tae employ me aince or twice and has peyed me well. She is a grand leddy an a credit tae ye.'

Sir Marmaduke continued to employ Geordie from time to time, but Geordie found it better to pay his yearly visit to her ladyship when her husband was absent. He managed it very discreetly and never once asked for more than £20. And still it all went to his mother for the upbringing and schooling of Jessie, who was growing into a very bonny and clever lassie, dark of hair and eyes, well mannered and devoted to her guardians.

Mrs Willison, who was still hale and capable, went out often to visit and help Kate at Brodie's country house. She sometimes took Jessie with her – this was not altogether wise, for the laird had a roving, indeed lustful eye and looked at this bonny black-eyed lass with desire. Jessie made no response at all, partly from discretion, for she had been well admonished by her guardian, partly from a sound, instinctive dislike of Brodie, and partly because she had become betrothed to an altogether estimable and attractive young man, William Forbes, clerk to one of the advocates in Parliament House. She told him about Brodie and gave up going to his house with Mrs Willison.

In mean resentment Brodie dismissed the Dempsters. He went further. Although he was on formal and distant terms with his uncle, he was much more at ease with Lady Maitland and found Louise a useful agent. Now he bribed her to spy on Jessie. He knew where Mrs Willison lived. Louise undertook this congenial task cunningly. She went cloaked and veiled, hung about the street and watched the comings and goings of Jessie, who noticed nothing. But Geordie did (and some thought Geordie saft!). Two can play at the game of disguise, and Geordie took that of a caddie. He bought himself a cloak such as other caddies wore, and a broad-brimmed hat, and he fixed a black patch over one eye. His mother and sister might have recognized him but not one who had seen him, as had Louise, only on infrequent occasions. Besides, Louise, although cunning, was also stupid.

Geordie spoke first. 'What are ye waitin for, mem?' he asked the lurking woman. As always he spoke politely. 'Can I tak a message for ye or dae ocht?'

'Do you live here, my good man?' asked the voice he knew.

'I dae that, an I wadna live onywhere else if ye peyed me.'

'Then can you tell me if a young woman, whose name is Jessie Warriston, lives up that stair. Do you know her by sight?'

'I ken her as weel as I ken mysel. Aye, she bides up that stair.'

'Ah good, that is excellent, that is what I want to know. You are a very good fellow, you have intelligence. I have something for you to do and you shall be well paid. Now tell me more – in that house where Jessie Warriston lives, is there also an idiot fellow called Geordie Willison. How long has Jessie lived there? Where does she comes from? What is her story?'

'Losh keep us, mem, ye ask owre mony questions a at once. Ye hae me fair confused. But I'll do my best to answer. Jessie has lived here seventeen years, a her life, wi that idiot Geordie Willison's mither. She's mebbe her granddochter. De ye no think sae yersel?'

'It is not for me to think. It is for you to find out and to tell me all you can. You will be paid well. Here is money now if you will take this letter to a gentleman, Ludovic Brodie, who lives some way outside the city. Do you know his name?'

'I ken his name, I ken whaur he bides. I'll tak the letter, thank ye kindly, mem,' as Louise handed him some money with the letter, and went off.

Geordie, who could not read, took the letter to his brother-in-law, Dempster, whom he told of the interview with the woman – but not that he knew her already. The letter had been written by Louise to Brodie, telling him that she had seen Jessie and had spoken to a caddie whom she would ask to deliver the letter. If he did, Mr Brodie might engage him, for sufficient payment to carry off the girl and deliver her to Brodie. This would give great satisfaction to Lady Maitland.

Hearing this, Geordie guessed that her ladyship had begun to suspect that the child was not dead but was known as Jessie Warriston, but that Brodie knew nothing of this. He desired merely to have the lass for his pleasure.

Dempster asked no questions, partly from discretion and partly because he had no need to, having guessed, in many a talk with Kate, the whole history. He and Geordie having made a plan, Geordie, still in cloak and wide-brimmed hat, the patch over one eye, went out to Brodie's house and delivered the letter introducing himself as one Peter Finlayson, a caddie.

'Well, my man, are you ready for a ploy* with a good bit of money in it?'

'I am that, sir. It'll no be the first. Ye may lippen* on Peter Finlayson for bauldness and discretion.'

'Well, then, tomorrow night you must bring Jessie to the resting-stone, the halt in Leith Walk. I shall be there with a carriage and there your work will end.'

'Mebbe, sir. But whit aboot the pay? Some wark may be paid efter it's dune, but it is, I'm thinkin, maun be peyed afore.'

'Very well; here is half your fee. The rest will be given you tomorrow when you bring the girl.'

'Verra gude, sir, an thank ye.'

Geordie counted the bonny gold guineas, stowed them carefully away and went back home.

He had made his plan with Dempster, who was happy to take part in anything against Brodie. Geordie told Jessie, a lass of spirit not easily frightened, that he had a ploy for her.

'Dinna be frichtit, ma lass. Juist sit quaiet. I'll be there.'

At the hour appointed, he was at the tryst with Jessie and found Brodie in his carriage.

'Here ye are, sir, an guid sport tae ye.'

Brodie laughed and gave him the rest of his fee. Geordie handed Jessie into the carriage, shut the door and fastened the handle with strong twine so that it could not be opened from the inside. Then he jumped up on the box, beside the coachman, landing so clumsily that he lurched and knocked the man's hat off.

'Ye clumsy lout! Get doon and gie me my bunnet.'

'What for wad I dae that? I'm a caddie, no an attendant on the likes of you.'

The man swore but clambered down, and Geordie seized the reins and drove off. 'Stop, ye rascal!' shouted the coachman running after. But he was heavy and slow, and Geordie drove fast.

'What's this! Stop, fellow!' shouted Brodie, his head out of the window.

'Aye, I'll stop sir, but no whaur ye expect.'

Geordie stopped outside a large building, undid the twine,

opened the door and handed Jessie out, took her on his arm and led her into a room where the sheriff appeared to be expecting them. Brodie followed. Dempster was also there, with a clerk and other witnesses.

'Mony thanks, my lord sheriff, for receiving me in this safe place – the jile. Ye ken my business, I hae informed yer lordship o the plot laid by Ludovic Brodie Esquire o Birkiehaugh, here present, and by the French leddy Louise Grécourt, to abduct this young leddy here, Jessie Warriston.'

It was all in order. The sheriff committed Brodie on the charge of abduction, and he was shortly afterwards tried and sentenced to six months imprisonment. Louise, at Geordie's request, was let off with an admonition.

She and Lady Maitland were badly frightened. They would have been more so had they known that Peter Finlayson and Geordie Willison were one and the same. Geordie now paid his usual call, making ironic apology for being later than usual. He intended no discourtesy.

'I hear that Sir Marmaduke's nephew Ludovic Brodie is jiled for trying tak awa the lassie Jessie Warriston. Nae doot that had yer leddyship's approval.' Silently Lady Maitland moved towards her bureau for Geordie's £20. 'Haud yer haun, leddy. I'm no beggin alms. I'm for daein you a service. I maun tell ye that the lassie Jessie bides wi my mither and has dune for the past seeventeen years. Wha her mither wis ma mither doesna ken, but she swears she maun hae been hangit, for the lassie has a dark ring, like that on a turtle dove, roond her bonny white neck. Is that no uncanny? Weel, leddy, it's like this. I hae vowed that ony man or wumman that tries tae herm the bonny lass, will suffer frae me. An noo I'll thank ye fir ma £20.'

The money was handed to him in silence, he bowed and departed.

The six months of Brodie's imprisonment had caused a fair amount of gossip and scandal not unmixed with pleasure, for that young man was not well liked. But the pleasure was mixed with pity for Sir Marmaduke. He, good man, had taken the disgrace very much to heart. He refused to see his nephew, and about the time of Brodie's release he died. Brodie, with his lawyer, made claim at once to the name and title of Maitland of Castle Gower and the estate of Sir Marmaduke.

Geordie was in frequent conference with Mr Carstairs, the advocate to whom young William Forbes, Jessie's sweetheart, was clerk. His mother, sister and brother-in-law wondered among themselves what the matter might be, but as usual they asked no questions. Then one day Geordie went out to Lady Maitland's house. He asked her to summon Louise, and spoke to them both.

'I hae heard wi regret that Sir Marmaduke is deid. He wis a gude man and true, and may the Lord reward him. I hae heard, forbye, that Ludovic Brodie, his nephew, is laying claim to the title and estate and his claim micht be granted if it's no opposed. But noo, my Leddy, I'm askin a favour o you. I'm askin yersel an Louise here to gang tae the coort and declare that you, ten months after yer husband went abroad, gave birth to a dochter, and that dochter is Jessie Warriston.'

Louise began chattering with rage. Lady Maitland spoke with dignity. 'Of that extraordinary statement you have no proof. This is the first time you have made it to me. I am guilty of no crime.'

'Indeed, my lady, he is mad, he is a fool. You should summon a footman and have him thrown downstairs.'

'Och, I'll gang awa gin ye bid me,' said Geordie calmly. 'I'll gang tae the coort masel and mak that statement. But I canna prove it unless I declare that yersel an the Frenchwumman here tried tae strangle the bairn an left it fir deid ahint yon high hedge at Warriston. An here is her leddyship's hair necklace which was twisted roun the puir bairn's neck an has left its mark.' He drew the necklace from his pocket. 'If ye declare the lass tae be yer dochter, my leddy. I'll say nocht aboot that. If ye dinna ye're lost. Baith o ye. Noo, will ye dae whit I ask?'

Louise shrieked in hysterics, Lady Maitland fainted. Geordie locked the door and stood looking calmly at both women. Presently Lady Maitland came to her senses, came to her feet and stood looking at Geordie.

'Be silent, Louise! Tell me, fellow, if I do as you demand, declare that this girl, Jessie Warriston, whom I've seen more than once, is my daughter whom I abandoned, you will do nothing more?'

Geordie gave his promise. He left the room and went quietly home.

On the day when Ludovic Brodie's claim was presented, another was made. This one was on behalf of Jessie Warrison or Maitland, as heiress to the late Sir George Maitland of Castle Gower. Brodie and his lawyer had no notion that this claim would be made. His claim, as next of kin, was about to be granted, when Lady Maitland and Louise entered the court. Geordie and Jessie, with his mother, Kate and her husband, were already present. Lady Maitland swore that Jessie was her daughter, born ten months after the departure of her husband abroad. Louise confirmed the declaration, having been present at the birth.

'That bastard,' sneered Brodie. 'Can ye take the word o a whore like her mother?'

He was sternly told to be silent. His lawyer more temperately pleaded that Jessie, being illegitimate and not the daughter of the late Sir Marmaduke, had no claim to be heiress to his name and title and estate. But it was declared and ruled that by the law of Scotland a child born in wedlock, ten months after the departure of the husband, was held to be legitimate offspring. Therefore it was found that Jessie Warriston was heiress and successor.

So the bonny lass took the name and title of Maitland of Castle Gower. Not long afterwards she added the name of Forbes when she married her sweetheart, William Forbes. There was both country and gentry at the wedding but the guests of honour were Geordie Willison, his mother, his sister and her husband.

And some thocht Geordie *saft*.

Source
John W. Wilson, *Tales of the Borders*, vol. 6, p. 93.

12   A Forger Foiled

William Wotherspoon was an eighteenth-century merchant in a village near Edinburgh. He was a man in his early thirties, greatly liked and respected for his integrity, kindness and gentle manners. He prospered in his business, and he thought of marriage. In this he chose well: the girl the daughter of a man of good family though of small means. That did not matter to Wotherspoon. What mattered was that Lucy had the good sense to value him and to return his love. Her family too liked him greatly. In fact, everyone was pleased – except one man, Lorimer.

Lorimer, the son of a farmer, had recently qualified in law but he was dissolute, selfish, lazy, a heartbreak to his good parents. He had wanted and wooed Lucy but she would have none of him. Now he was filled with bitter hatred and jealousy of Wotherspoon and of rancour against Lucy. He brooded and plotted revenge.

The marriage was happy, children were born and were a delight to their parents, Wotherspoon's affairs prospered. Then, through no fault of his own, disaster struck. The bank into which he had invested his savings failed. This failure involved many people. It hit Wotherspoon hard but he took it bravely, and so did his wife. He continued in business, lived frugally and gradually paid off his creditors. They all respected and trusted him, and they did not press him. Gradually, bit by bit, he paid them.

Among the last to be paid was a commercial traveller, and when Wotherspoon had saved enough to make full payment, they met at an inn to celebrate, with a good supper and a good wine – rather too much perhaps of the wine, for Wotherspoon became garrulous and even boastful.

'There's my last debt paid but ane,' he told his creditor. 'I'm still awin £50 but that will be paid as sune as I can, even if I have tae tak tae the road an haud up a coach or twa, or put my name to a bit o paper.'

'Ye'll no dae that, I'm thinkin,' the traveller told him, chuckling.

They parted on the happiest of terms and Wotherspoon went home. The next day he went to business and continued his douce, decent way of life.

A few days later his wife was standing at the shop door with her baby in her arms when a post chaise, driven at speed, stopped opposite. One man descended, the other followed him after hitching the reins to a post. As they came over to Mrs Wotherspoon, she called to her husband, 'They're comin here, Will,' and he came out of the shop.

'Is your name William Wotherspoon?' demanded one of the men.

'It is.'

The man drew a paper from his pocket. 'William Wotherspoon, we arrest you in the name of the King. You will accompany us to Edinburgh.'

'Me! Ye canna arrest me. I've no done naethin against the King and the Law.'

'So ye say. But ye're here charged wi forgery.'

'My man guilty o forgery! It's a black lee an a slander. He's guilty o nae faut,' declared his wife stoutly.

'If that is so, then he will return a free man, but he must face the charge in coort.'

The men were implacable. There was nothing for it but to obey. William went with them quietly and utterly bewildered. He comforted his wife, 'Dinna greet, lass, I maun gang wi them but I'll be back sune eneuch.'

But he was long in coming. In Edinburgh he was committed to prison, and brought to trial on a charge of forgery – which at that time was a capital offence.

His poor wife was in sore grief. The neighbours tried to comfort her: 'There's been a blunder' or 'It's a some dreadfu mistake, a gey queer mistake, but it'll a come richt at the trial.'

Wotherspoon himself knew that there was some queer mistake – but how had it come about? When he came up for trial at the High Court, the charge against him was that he had forged a bill for £50 in the name of a farmer Laidlaw. His accuser was Lorimer, who stated upon oath that Wotherspoon had then made the bill payable to him, Lorimer, for professional services.

The bill from Laidlaw was in payment of goods as supplied by Wotherspoon to the farmer.

Lorimer further deponed that he had taken the bill to a bank in Edinburgh. Shortly afterwards he had called at the bank and asked for a private interview with the manager. He told him gravely that he now believed, and had good reason to believe, that the bill was a forgery, perpetrated by Wotherspoon.

Wotherspoon continued to declare his innocence and, indeed, his ignorance of the affair. He did not know Laidlaw, had never supplied him with any goods and had never employed the services of Lorimer.

Lorimer declared that he had given Wotherspoon his professional services at the time of his bankruptcy and that the bill had been endorsed and given to him when he and the prisoner met at a tavern in Edinburgh kept by James Bryce and his wife – a most respectable couple, their inn having a good name. They averred that they had seen the panel with Lorimer on a certain evening in September. All this Wotherspoon steadfastly denied. He had not been in Edinburgh on that day or indeed on any day.

One witness called was his shopman, Anderson, who was shown the bill and asked if this were truly his master's signature.

'It's like it, but I canna be sure. I canna swear tae it.' Asked if he knew whether his master had employed Lorimer, he declared that he did not know. Asked further if that meant that Lorimer had not been so employed or that he might have been employed without the knowledge of the witness or deponent, Anderson agreed that the latter suggestion might be true – but he did not know. This was of no help to the prosecution but of little help to the defence.

A second witness, Andrew Hislop, swore upon oath that Wotherspoon had told him that he had employed Lorimer and had paid him £50 with an endorsed bill of that amount.

The most credible witnesses were the innkeeper and his wife. They swore to having seen Wotherspoon with Lorimer, sitting with him at a table. He had been asked to sit with them, had seen Wotherspoon endorse and hand over the bill to Lorimer and had heard him say with relief that that was the last of his debts.

Finally Lorimer, with apparent reluctance, told the court of having overheard Wotherspoon's boast to the commercial traveller that he had only one debt left to pay, one of £50, and

that he would pay it if he had to hold up a coach or put his name
to a bit of paper. This foolish speech outweighed all the evidence
in the panel's favour, that of his respectable reputation and
honourable behaviour.

Wotherspoon's counsel, a young advocate named Moffat, did
his best, fortified by his own conviction of his client's innocence,
but the weight of evidence was against him. Wotherspoon was
found guilty, sentenced to be hanged and taken back to prison.

There was much sympathy with him, but the verdict was
approved by the directors of the bank where Lorimer had
presented and cashed the bill. By a strict reading of the law,
Lorimer might have been held at least in part guilty, but the
directors were so pleased with the verdict, and with his reporting
his suspicion, that they not only forbore to make any charge but
paid him the amount with something added.

Wotherspoon's only comfort was his knowledge of his innocence, and his faith in a judge of a justice and authority beyond
all earthly standards who would vindicate him.

His counsel, young Moffat, was unhappy and perplexed. He
could not accept the guilt of his client; he was a perceptive young
man and he felt, though he could not prove or even clearly argue
it, that there was something wrong about the whole case. He did
his best to comfort the prisoner.

When the trial ended, Moffat went into the country to stay
with a friend who was a laird. They walked in the garden of the
house where two men were working. As they came near, one of
the men looked up at Moffat, said something to the other, threw
up his spade and ran off.

'What ails Andrew Hislop?' the laird asked the gardener.

'I dinna ken, sir, but he said something about having been
witness in a case whaur this gentleman [indicating Moffat] was
pleadin; that it was a gey queer case, and that if he himsel hadna
stuck firm to what he deponed, anither might have swung for the
crime. But he didna want to be asked questions, sir, an he thocht
ye wad ask owre many.'

'Well might he say that,' declared Moffat. 'I remember him
now. His name, his declaration that Wotherspoon, my poor and
still respected client, had told him of having employed Lorimer
and having paid him £50. I must speak again to this Hislop.'

'We'll send after him.' said the laird, and at once he

despatched his servants. Andrew had not yet gone beyond pursuit, and he was brought back.

The laird was a justice of the peace so it was all done in order. Andrew Hislop was taken under guard to Edinburgh and lodged in the Edinburgh Tolbooth, the Heart of Midlothian, where he collapsed completely and made his confession. The glimmer of suspicion which Moffat had seen became a clear light. The guilty man was not his good and honest client but his accuser – Lorimer.

Hislop confirmed this. He poured out his confession. Lorimer had come to him suggesting that he impersonate Wotherspoon. There was a distinct resemblance between them – as Moffat saw – and this had given Lorimer his plan. Hislop met him in Edinburgh at the Bryces' inn, was handed the bill bearing Laidlaw's forged signature – forged skilfully by Lorimer – and added a fair imitation of Wotherspoon's. The innkeeper and his wife had been easily deceived by the likeness between Hislop and Wotherspoon, both seen for the first time and seen only once. Lorimer had promised to give his accomplice £10. He gave him only five.

Young Moffatt took it all down, Hislop signed, and his signature was witnessed. A re-trial was ordered. Wotherspoon appeared, behaving with his usual dignity and composure. He wore his wig, as he had always worn it. The Lord Advocate ordered that it should be placed on the head of Andrew Hislop, who had just made his full confession. Bryce and his wife were again called as witnesses and bidden to look at both men. They realized their mistake, one very easily made. It was indeed Hislop who had sat at the table with Lorimer and signed the bill with the name of William Wotherspoon.

Wotherspoon was declared innocent with more than formality – with warm sympathy and admiration for his fortitude. There was applause in court which their lordships on the bench seemed in no hurry to suppress.

It had all happened so quickly that Lorimer had no warning, no time, in which to attempt to escape. He was arrested, tried for perjury and forgery, sentenced and, within a few days, hanged in the Grassmarket. In admitting his guilt he told the court that the idea had come to him from overhearing, in the village inn, Wotherspoon's foolish boast that he would pay his sole

The Grass Market looking west

remaining debt if he had to take to highway robbery or to putting his name to a bit of paper – to forgery.

William Wotherspoon returned home to his good wife. There was much rejoicing in the village and countryside. Did she utter any reproach for the boast? Probably not, for she was a gentle creature. There was no need for anyone to reprove William, for he blamed his own folly severely, and never again did he so miscall himself.

Source
John J. Wilson, *Tales of the Borders*

13   The Warlock of the West Bow

Of Major Thomas Weir, the warlock of the West Bow, Stevenson has written memorably but too briefly; Scott was fascinated by him – in 1809, five years before the publication of *Waverley*, he wrote in a letter: 'If ever I were to become a writer of romances, I think I would choose Major Weir, if not for my hero, at least for an agent in my production.'

The Major was indeed an agent – of evil, and he haunted the city long after his own dark day. As Stevenson has recorded, 'Old Edinburgh cannot clear herself of his memory', and Weir may be held one of the most evil citizens of a city which has never lacked evildoers of notorious fame.

A citizen but not a native of Edinburgh, Thomas Weir was born near Carluke in Lanarkshire in 1599; his mother was 'a sorceress of repute'. He was an officer in Leslie's Covenanting army, fighting against that man Charles Stuart who was little better than a Papist and his adherent and champion Montrose. That was the language and action approved in Calvinistic Lanarkshire.

Weir and his sister Jean, a witch like their mother before them, lived in a house at the West Bow which Robert Chambers described as 'a curious whimsical-looking street of great steepness and narrowness, between the Low and High Town, a passage for the entry of sovereigns' – those sovereigns including, in the Major's time, that potent Lord of Hell to whom he gave allegiance.

The Major and his sister were celebrated for their piety among the members of an exclusive and godly sect, the Bowhead Saints. His knowledge of Scripture was prodigious, his fervour in prayer so notable that he was known as Angelical Thomas. At their meetings he always prayed standing upright, leaning on a staff without which he was never seen to move, although the legend says that the staff was sometimes seen without him. It went on errands, it opened the door like a footman. It was black and

The West Bow from the Lawn Market

heavily carved with figures of satyrs and the like. The Major himself was tall and dark, with 'a grim countenance and a big nose', and he 'ordinarily looked down to the ground.' His sister was, in Stevenson's phrase, 'a marvellous spinster' – or spinner, which was not, in her, a sign of virtuous industry.

If not yet revered as Angelical Thomas, Weir was greatly respected. A woman, too observant for her own good, once reported to the magistrates of Lanark some uncanny and dark behaviour of his that she had seen one night in a field. Her charge was not accepted and she was sentenced to be whipped through the town for her evil speaking against this godly defender of truth and righteousness. Her vindication would come and be, no doubt, very sweet.

In Edinburgh, the Major (the rank with which he retired from the army) became Captain of the City Guard, predecessors of the police. An early biographer, Sinclair, has recorded that he was 'very active in discovering and reprehending the Cavaliers, and bringing them to be arraigned and try'd for their lives' and he was the glory of that peculiar sect the Bowhead Saints for this activity as for his piety. His modern biographer, William

Roughead, has commented: '. . . though in his day a stalwart of the Covenant . . . for obvious reasons finds no place in the Presbyterian martyrology.'

As Captain of the Guard and prison warder Weir showed a particular and subtle cruelty to the captured Royalist general Montrose, of whom he had charge in captivity. He kept him in a dark cell lit by one candle, visiting the cell frequently, smoking heavily, knowing that the fumes sickened Montrose. He mocked him, calling him 'dog' and 'atheist', taunting him that God as well as man had forsaken him.

In the City Guard Weir had authority. His contract with the Devil gave him both power and protection, for Satan takes care of his own – up to a point. This contract included his being defended against all mischance, 'except one Burn.' He took the warning very much to heart. One night on his rounds as captain he found the Netherbow unguarded and went in search of the delinquents. He found them in an ale-house and when he denounced them they pleaded that they had left their posts only for a few minutes, to drink with an old crony, one Burn. As that name was spoken, the Major started and shuddered. He went straight home and did not emerge from his house for some days.

For a long time things went well with the Major, esteemed, even revered among the Bowhead Saints.

Of his sister, who kept house for him, there is a particular legend which would seem to come from fairy lore, one of those encounters with the Other People, the elves, fauns and fairies who are neither of humankind nor of the Devil.

Miss Jean had for a time kept a school in Dalkeith. There she was once visited by a woman who begged her to speak and intercede on her behalf with the Queen of the Fairies. Next day another woman appeared, a tiny creature who gave Jean 'a piece of a tree or root', an amulet and much silver. When this benefactress had departed, Jean found her spindle full of fine yarn, more than she or anyone could have spun in that time.

No tongues wagged against Major Weir and his sister. He held his godly audience enthralled. One of his biographers, the Very Reverend George Hickes, Dean of Worcester, wrote of him in 1678 that he had 'a particular gracefulness in whining and sighing above any of the sacred clan, and had learned to deliver himself upon all serious occasions in a far more ravishing accent than any of the ministers could attain unto.' This favour continued until the first act of the drama came, suddenly, startlingly.

The congregation were in session, and the Major rose to address them. He stood, leaning on his staff, a necessary support, for he had been gravely ill and looked ghastly. He began to speak, emitting not the expected eloquence of prayer but a confession of appalling inhuman sins. The congregation sat as if bound by a most evil spell. (And this report comes from no ignorant gossip but from a learned source, the Reverend George Sinclair, Professor of Philosophy in the University of Glasgow, in his treatise *Satan's Invisible World Discovered*.)

The Major ended his confession: 'Before God, I have not told even the hundreth part of that I can say and am guilty of.'

There followed a conspiracy of silence and concealment, mingled with incredulity. But there was one exception: a minister, who reported the matter to the Lord Provost, Sir Andrew Ramsay, an advocate and later Senator of the College of Justice. He at first took no legal action – through sheer incredulity. His legal mind considered the Major to be full of delusions, and he sent doctors to examine him. When they pronounced him sound in body and mind, the Provost sent clergy, who agreed with the medical verdict, but found that 'the terrors of God were upon his soul' and urged confession. Legal action was now inevitable. The City Guard were sent to arrest the Major, his sister and the black staff – on which the Major confirmed his dependence. Lodged in the Tolbooth, did the former Captain of the Guard remember Montrose in his dark cell, sickened by tobacco fumes, mocked and taunted?

The two bailies* who had commanded the Guard returned to the Major's house and collected some packets of money, wrapped in rags. They adjourned to a tavern where they put all the money into one bag, tossing the rags into the fire, where they did not burn quietly but rose circling as in a dance, then exploding.

After her arrest, Jean babbled. She told about their witch mother and about their allegiance to Satan, and the favours he granted them. One night in September 1648 he had sent a fiery coach to carry them to Musselburgh and back, and had told them of the defeat of the Scots army at Preston some days before the news reached Edinburgh. She told, too, that strange tale of her fairy visitor at Dalkeith.

The year was 1670: the King had come into his own again, and Episcopacy had been restored in Scotland. The Bishop and the Dean of Edinburgh offered spiritual aid but were refused. As Robert Chambers has reported, with a hint of amazement or amusement, 'Even the offer of a Presbyterian clergyman, instead of an established Episcopal minister of the city, had no effect upon him.' Weir chose impenitence. To every request that he would pray, he answered in screams: 'Torment me no more – I am tormented enough already.' Again to quote Robert Chambers: While the wretched man lay in prison, he made no scruple to disclose the particulars of his guilt, but refused to address himself to the Almighty for pardon.

They were tried, the witch and the warlock, in April 1670, before two Justices-Depute, William Murray and John Preston. Counsel for the prosecution was the Lord Advocate himself, Sir John Nisbet. There was no counsel for the defence. Four witnesses were called from the congregation that had heard that dreadful confession. Finally both accused admitted their guilt. Doom was pronounced. Jean was to be hanged in the Grassmarket, the Major to be taken to the Gallows Lee between Edinburgh and Leith and there strangled at the stake, then burned. His staff was to be burned with him – the staff 'without which he could not pray or work any of his diabolical feats', as Sinclair reports, adding that '. . . whatever incantation was in it, the persons present own it gave rare burning, and was long to burn, as also himself.'

In dying, Weir declared that he had no hope of any mercy. According to Dean Hickes, it was claimed '. . . by very credible persons that the body of this unclean Beast gave many manifest tokens of its impurity . . . as soon as it began to be heated'. William Roughead has suggested that the Major may have been burned alive.

An account of his death was taken by a minister to Jean, who was awaiting her own execution. Her chief concern was for the staff. She fell on her knees, not in grief or penitence but in rage, 'uttering words horrible to remember.' The minister, with more than a little discretion and more than a little reprobation, stopped her outpourings, which were horrifying or delighting a crowd of onlookers. Then she declared that she would die 'with all the shame she could.' This the good cleric took to mean remorse, but it was far from that.

On the scaffold she threw off her cloak, 'her gown-tayle, and was purposed to cast off all her cloaths before all the multitude.'

The bailie in charge of the business ordered the executioner to proceed. When the man was about to throw her from the ladder, she struck him in the face, her hands not having been tied, and tried to free herself. She was overcome and hanged by the neck until she was dead.

The life and death of Major Weir are black with diabolic magic. About the witch's end there is an element, hardly less fearful, of black comedy.

Stevenson, who should have made them actors in a book, not merely figures in a sketch however brilliant, wrote: 'Whether these two were simply religious maniacs of the more furious order, or had real as well as imaginary sins upon their old-world shoulders, are points happily beyond the reach of our intention.' Happily? We might have found, if not happiness, a strange enthralment in reading a Stevenson masterpiece about the witch and the warlock of the West Bow. And many who lived through the Second World War and heard accounts of Hitler's evil-doing in Germany and Stalin's in Russia are not inclined to scepticism about the Devil and his mastery over the bodies, minds and souls of men.

The memory, the legend, the myth (for legend and myth are half-compact of truth) long outlived the witch and warlock. According to Stevenson, '. . . the facts struck the public fancy, and brought forth a remarkable family of myths', of the haunted house, lit by night, of 'gigantic females laughing and gaping with "tehees of laughter"' who haunted the West Bow. He himself had been told by his father, that he, Thomas, had '. . . often been told in the nursery how the Devil's coach, drawn by six coal-black horses with fiery eyes, would drive at night into the West Bow, and belated people might see the Major through the glasses.'

It was a tradition that once a year there was a night's release from Hell for witch and warlock, driven to their house at midnight, taken up again in the small hours of the morning, that there was revelry in that house, windows lit, shadowy figures seen come and go.

Such a vision was seen by a douce, homely woman who had been visiting her niece and newborn baby. As she walked home, about midnight, attended by a maidservant carrying a lantern, there appeared at the windows of the warlock's house three women, shouting uproariously, shrieking with eldritch laughter. The good wife and her maid walked on steadily. At the door of the house they were met by an immense, phantasmal female shaking with hideous laughter. When they came to a lane commonly called Stinking Close (in the Edinburgh of *gardy-loo** the stink must have been almost audible and visible to be thus noted), they saw the house ablaze with lights, heard it raucous with laughter. The two brave women fled – to the safety of home.

But the apparitions continued. The staff appeared, opening the door like an attentive footman. The coach and six galloped to the Bowhead and away again when the hours of leave were over. By one account the horses were headless, and so was the coachman. It carried the witch and the warlock to their infernal revels, back to their own place with their master.

Source
Robert Chambers, *Traditions of Edinburgh*, pp. 26, 31–7

14 The Major's Coach

The legend of the warlock Major lingered into the next century, into the age of reason, culture, commonsense and this-worldliness. The phantasmal figure may not have been seen, the staff may not have walked the street or opened the door, but it was frequently reported that the black coach drawn by six black horses was driven to the West Bow. From the legend grew incidents.

Modern Edinburgh was being developed in the New Town. Among its chief makers was Lord Provost Drummond, greatly admired by many, condemned and opposed by a faction, particularly in the matter of building a bridge over the Nor Loch to be a way between the old town and the new.

Among the opponents were two members of the Guild or Incorporation of Cabinet Makers, Dickson the deacon, and Thomas Kerr the treasurer, who was hoping to succeed Dickson as deacon at the next election. One night they discussed the matter of the new bridge and various other concerns at a private session in an ale house in the High Street, kept by one Luckie Bell. This house was noted for the quantity and quality of its ale and whisky.

The two men had drunk freely and emerged cheerfully if not over-steadily as the clock of St Giles was striking its quarters. It proceeded to strike the hour of midnight. It was September, and there was a harvest moon which threw a bright radiance over part of the street but left many shadows under the tall, dark 'lands' (tenements).

'Gude keep us, it's twal o the clock,' said Kerr. 'We've been owre lang in Luckie Bell's an drunk owre much o her ale.'

'But think on the business we've done thegither. We've settled maitters aboot the Guild and we may weel hae put a spoke in the Provost's wheel. Him and his bridge, the Deil fly awa wi it.'

'That's a verra weel,' said Kerr gloomily, 'but it's noo the morn's morn,* an whit am I tae say tae my wife?'

'Och, whit need ye fear frae her?' said Dickson carelessly, his own wife being a quiet creature not given to flyting.* 'It's time that man Drummond was put down. I'll wager it was him that set yon masons to pu doun my outside stair. I sent them aboot their business. I had two o the Toun Guaird tak them to the magistrate but they were dismissed wi an admonition an noo I've been ordered no to build it up again, but to pu it doun an build it up again inside.' His voice changed suddenly to one of amazement. 'Are ye listenin, man? Are ye asleep that ye dinna see what I see, a high bricht wa across the High Street that wasna there this mornin. It wasna there when we set oot.'

'Aye I see it, a high white wa.* This cowes a.* It's no canny. The Provost has dune this, sent his masons; there maun hae been a hundred o them to dae the wark sae quickly.'

'He's dune it to spite me,' declared the deacon. 'I've a gude mind to ca oot the Guaird an hae it pu'ed doun – I could start tae pu it doun wi my ain hauns.'

'Canny noo,' advised Kerr as the pair of them lurched towards St Giles and Parliament Square. In front of them was a flood of moonlight reaching up to the second storey of the high lands. This, to their ale-fuddled vision, was the new wall.

'We'll no can win hame that wey,' said the treasurer. 'Let's turn doon Fishmarket Close an up the Coogate tae the West Bow.'

'An I'll see to the business in the mornin.' This agreed, they staggered on and came at last to Dickson's house and his patient, anxious wife, to whom they told the whole story, which the good woman received with sympathy, credulity and amazement. She soothed him with good words and a posset and they went to bed. The treasurer continued his way home with small hope of a similar kind reception from his wife. She had a sharp tongue and used it freely.

Early in the morning Mrs Dickson, a good housewife, rose and went to the well at the Bowhead to draw her buckets of water. Other women were gathering there and she told them her amazing story. 'Losh, keep me. D'ye tell me that!'

'Awa, ye couldna build a wa in that time.'

'Let's gae doun an see.'

They all trooped off down to St Giles, squat and solid, to the Luckenbooths, to Parliament Square with Parliament Hall, the centre of the law, the home of pleaders and advocates and

Parliament House

judges. They looked round, and laughed. No trace of a wall was to be seen. It was all exactly as it had been, as they had always known it, a centre of law and business, kirk and market, with the tall lands looking down. The women laughed hilariously.

'Och, Luckie Dickson, whaur wiz yer gude man yestreen? He maun hae been gey fu.' Their laughter was not bitter or unkindly mocking, for the deacon's wife was well liked and her man respected, and they all knew what ale could do to their own husbands' wits.

The matter did not end there. The women gave up teasing Mrs Dickson but they took the tale back to their husbands, who relished it. For a time it was one of the town jokes.

'We needna gang hame yet,' a man would say to his cronies. 'We can drink anither cup o ale or maybe twa afore we're likely to see the deacon's moon wa.'

As for Thomas Kerr the treasurer, his way was hard. He was walking home somewhat gloomily, dreading the encounter with his sharp-tongued wife, when he heard the sound of weeping and saw, sitting on the wall of a well, an old woman he knew well, the Widow Horner. Her husband and his own father had been good friends and neighbours, both prosperous, rather more so than himself and the widow's son. He had heard gossip that the old mother was not well treated.

'Whit ails ye, Mistress? Whit are ye daein here at this hour o the nicht or mornin?'

'Speir nae questions, Tammas Kerr. Gang ye're weys an leave me tae my grief.'

'I canna leave ye yer lane. Lat me tak ye hame.'

'I hae nae hame. My son has turned me oot. His wife bade him dae it. They winna hae me. I hae nae hame, leave me noo, lat me dee.'

Thomas stood miserably beside her. Part of his mind bade him do as she bade – it was not his affair; part of him was deep in compassion and in shame, for he could not reproach the widow's son with callous behaviour as he was near committing the same sin. His wife was at him continually to turn his own old mother out of the house. There had never been friendship between them. Old Mrs Kerr was or had been partly to blame. She had not liked or welcomed her daughter-in-law and had shown at first that she thought her inferior. This had never been forgiven, although the old woman had tried to overcome her dislike, to conceal her feelings, and had been polite and quiet enough. But the nagging went on and, as Thomas was not of a very strong character, of late he had not been kind to his mother. With that burden on his conscience, he walked unhappily and guiltily away. He tried to excuse himself. His mother was aye greetin and girnin,* his wife aye at him to put her away; there was no peace for him in his own house. It had been the same with Rab Horner – and who was Thomas to blame him, and what could he do?

As he walked back, he could hear the crunch of wheels.

'Major Weir's coach,' he told himself; it was said still to be driven up the street with its black horses. Now it would follow him, and what might happen? He might be lifted and taken away. It would be the punishment for his weakness and heartless behaviour. He must do penance.

As the sound came nearer, he dashed into a dark doorway and crouched at the foot of some stairs. The coach stopped, the door opened, feet rushed up the stairs, rushed down again, he was seized and carried out and thrust into the coach.

'Lord have mercy upon my sinful soul,' groaned poor Thomas

and sank into a swoon. When he came to himself, he found himself seated in the coach between two dark figures, both headless – their heads were swinging from the roof. He tried to slip onto the floor but was grasped firmly and painfully by each arm. A deep, harsh voice spoke.

'Be still. Make no cry for help, for none will hear you. Speak no words but those of confession and contrition. The Major will be your judge. He knows the blackness of your heart.'

Thomas began to recall everything he had ever done wrong: the sins committed, the good left undone, above all his neglect of his old mother, his cruelty, his cowardice in letting his wife have her way. His face was wet with tears of contrition. This was surely the very moment of death. He was silent. The coach stopped. The voice spoke again, 'Thomas Kerr, your contrition has saved you. Your sins are many and dark, you have been a bad and cruel son. Cease not to repent and to make amends while there is still time. Now go!'

The door was opened and he was thrust roughly out. He fell on the ground, upon wet grass, and heard the coach driven rapidly away. It was dark, with no light of the moon. It was cold and the rain dripped down upon him. He rose and stumbled onto some stones and waited – waited for the first glimmer of dawn, waited for any sound to break the deadly silence. A wind blew, bitterly cold. He would die of cold before he was found, if he did not die of terror. Then the dawn appeared in the sky, the rain ceased and Thomas thanked God in His mercy for sparing him. Far off in the distance there came the sound of horses' hooves, accompanied by the friendly slow roll of wheels and a cheerful whistle.

'Stop! Stop!' Thomas cried. 'Stop an tak me up.'

'No likely,' was the rough answer. 'Bide whaur ye are. If ye try tae stop me, I'll set ma dug on ye.'

'But please stop an tak me up, tak me hame. I'm lost and near deid wi the cauld. I'm nae gangrel* body, I'm Thomas Kerr, carpenter and cabinet-maker. I'll reward ye well but tak me hame.'

The cart stopped. A dog growled. 'Wheesht noo, Bauldy. Is it you Tammas Kerr that has a shop in St Mary's Wynd?'

'Aye, it is. An what's yer ain name?'

'I'm Wattie Clinkscale, the cairrier fae North Berwick, on my wey tae the toun. I come ilka* week. Come up and I'll tak ye hame. But whit brings ye oot here sae faur frae the toun at sic an hour. Ye should hae been in yer bed twa or three hours ago. I doobt ye've been at a guild dinner. It maun has been a gude ane, owre gude for yer ane gude.'

Wattie laughed at his own wit. He held a hand to help Kerr climb up. Wattie was a decent fellow and asked no questions. As the light grew stronger, he drove into the city and set Thomas down near his own door. Thomas walked feebly to his house. It was opened to him by his mother, who looked sad and anxious.

'O my bairn, my puir laddie. Whaur hae ye been? Ye're hauf deid wi the cauld. Come in, come in an sit ye doun by the fire till I mak ye a hot toddy, syne awa tae yer bed. Ye're fair forfoughan.'*

The gentle voice nearly broke her son's heart. He wept, he kissed the kind old face, held her in his arms.

'Mither, Mither, forgive me a the ill I hae done ye.'

'Ye've done me nae ill, my puir laddie.'

'Aye, but I have and I repent it sair, but I'll mak amends. Mither, Mither, say ye forgie me an gie me yer blessin.'

'My bairn, my bairn, if ye hae dune me ony ill – which I canna think – I forgie ye an bless ye a thoosand times ower in the name o God and the Blessed Saviour.'

As Thomas knelt before her, she laid her hand on his head, then made him rise and sit by the fire. 'Och my bonny laddie, ye've made me a happy wumman the nicht. Noo sit ye doun an warm yersel.'

She prepared and brought him a fine hot toddy with honey in it, and a bannock. 'Noo awa tae yer bed.' And he obeyed her.

His wife had awakened and was ready to question and to scold but his mother, with a new authority, bade her to be silent and to leave her man to sleep. Thomas added in a tone his wife had never heard before. 'Aye, haud yer tongue. Lat my mither be, an nae mair o yer flyting. She is here to bide an ye will treat her wi respect. Noo, lat me be. I maun sleep.'

He slept late into the afternoon and awoke somewhat refreshed, but his foolish, ill-natured wife would not hold her tongue and it made him feverish. He slept again but fitfully and woke confused. A doctor was sent for. Thomas was worse: he was raving now, his mind was full of the terror of the black coach of Major Weir. Wattie the carrier came to ask for him and tell where and how he had found him. The tale spread and was believed by many, for the legend of the Major's black, diabolic coach was still strong. Others had heard the furious galloping horses but had not dared to look out.

It was not only the credulous who believed. The matter was taken seriously by responsible citizens, including the Provost himself and the magistrates. They believed that some mischief had been, and perhaps was still being planned, not diabolic but all the same lawless, and the Town Guard, of which the warlock had once been a captain, were ordered to keep watch. But nothing more was seen or heard.

Thomas Kerr began to improve under the care of his wise doctor and good mother. Maybe the doctor spoke his mind to the nagging wife, ordering her to leave her man in peace, and commended the gentleness and devotion of the old mother. Thomas himself spoke once but effectively.

'My mither is tae bide wi us and hae the honour paid that is her due. Mind that and nae mair o yer flytin.' His wife was astonished into submission. And this too became known. Rab Horner followed the good example, shamed into decency, and brought his mother back to his house.

The elections drew near. Deacon Dickson was active in canvassing for himself and his chosen colleagues. Kerr withdrew his candidature for the office of deacon. Dickson was not re-elected, a disappointment which he took very well; Kerr was again appointed treasurer, which proved an excellent tonic. There was a supper of celebration at which the new deacon and his predecessor sat together very amicably. There was a good deal of talk, some deploring the building of the new bridge, but it was now accepted. Healths were drunk, including that of Treasurer Kerr, and shortly before midnight, for next day was the Sabbath, the company left their tavern, walking in procession two and two, the former and the new deacon together, arm in arm, one of them drunk, all of them mellow.

They trundled up the High Street and down the Cowgate, and they heard the sound of coach wheels and of horses hooves. Then, to their amazement, came the black coach driven fast, the fearsome black horses, the coachman headless, with his head held in one hand. Dickson, never a coward and now emboldened by drink and by outrage, jumped and seized the reins, as did his companion the new deacon. The coachman threw his head at Dickson, who held grimly on; the head returned to its owner and was thrown again, and from the windows flew other heads. Both deacons held fast; the others ran after the coach; the heads flew and returned to their owners.

At the foot of College Wynd the coach stopped, the coachman leaped down, rushed off and disappeared. The doors opened: another two dark, headless figures leaped out and followed the coachman. Our band of twelve good men and true took possession and made discoveries, joined by some neighbours, roused and inquisitive. On the box they found a greatcoat with a contraption of basketwork above the shoulders, a frame which hid the head of the wearer. Attached to it by a long cord was the artificial, life-like head that had been thrown. Inside the coach were two similar contraptions with heads. It was clear how the trickery had been played – on them and on Thomas Kerr, and how the perpetrators had escaped.

The coach was packed with packages which were not in the least terrifying or uncanny, only illegal: bales of rich silk, boxes of fine tea and good tobacco, a source of considerable revenue which somehow never reached the authorities.

It was noted in the months to come that many a good housewife appeared at the kirk in a fine silk gown such as she had never before worn; that there were tea-drinkings when the ladies of that quarter enjoyed the most exquisite China tea; that men smoked unusually good tobacco. It was all most elegant and genteel. There was gossip with much guessing but no tongue wagged in that city of tongue-waggers. Many folk enjoyed a little gift of tea or tobacco or a silk scarf.

Some of the treasure was taken by Dickson to Thomas Kerr that very afternoon and proved, along with his narrative, the final cure: a length of silk for his wife who did not deserve it, one for his mother who did; tea for both of them and tobacco for the treasurer. He listened, and for the first time since his collapse he laughed.

Thereafter things went well with both friends. Thomas Kerr proved himself master in his own house, his wife submitted and, being not altogether bad at heart, made life comfortable for her mother-in-law. As for that mild woman Mrs Dickson, it is likely

St Giles Church, County Hall and Lawn Market, High Street

that she went so far as to put her husband in his place from time to time, reminding him of that miracle of the moon wall. Both men prospered in business.

One day a few years later an elderly man in seaman's dress, shabby and poor, came to Kerr's shop asking for work. He had, he said, served an apprenticeship in youth. Kerr was glad to employ him for he needed good hands, and he found this man diligent and efficient, no 'prentice hand. One day he came to old Mrs Kerr and asked. 'Mem, d'ye mind o Wattie Brown?'

'Losh, deed I do. Is it yersel? It's been a lang time. But now ye tell me I kin see the laddie in ye. It wis a daft thing ye did, but ye needna hae run awa. How hae ye fared?'

'Aye, it was daft and I've repented it. But noo I'm hame an I gie ye my word I'll serve your son better than I served his faither, wha was a gude maister to me.'

Wattie told his whole story. It had begun with the Porteous Riots which had set Edinburgh in a lather. John Porteous had been one of the most hated men in the city. As Captain in the City Guard, he had captured and held one Wilson, a smuggler, whom he treated with appalling cruelty before his execution and on the scaffold. There was a riot among the crowd, especially among the apprentices. Porteous fired and killed a man, then permitted or ordered his men to fire other shots. He himself was taken and, by popular clamour, brought to trial, found guilty and himself condemned to be hanged. Then, at the eleventh hour came a reprieve. The fire of hatred and revenge, already smouldering, never extinguished, blazed up. The mob of apprentices rushed the Tolbooth, Wattie among them. When the door proved too firmly barred, he rushed back to his master's shop, took a heavy hammer and with that broke down the door. The mob rushed in, seized Porteous and carried him off to his doom.

Sickened by the ferocity of their vengeance and in great fear, Wattie was on his way home when a stranger spoke to him, giving him a golden guinea 'for the good work you have done' and bidding him, 'if you find yourself in trouble for this night's work, make your way to Anstruther, where you will find help.'

The stranger disappeared. Wattie went back to his room and his bed, but not to sleep. After a few hours of misery he rose and slipped out of the house. And there he met again the stranger, now followed by some twelve men. 'So you need my help. Well, we're all on our way to Anstruther. Follow me.'

He led them out of the city through Holyrood Park to Duddingston. There, on the shore, two boats were drawn up. The party embarked and sailed to Anstruther in Fife, where they transferred to larger, cargo vessel. Thence they sailed to Holland, carrying a large cargo, all of it duly declared and lawful, then on to Antwerp. And so began the years of exile for Wattie Brown, employed about the trading business between Scotland and the Low Countries, using his craft as a carpenter, always busy. He had comrades and he lived well, like a good Scot putting aside some part of his wages.

'But I was aye homesick for Scotland, for Auld Reekie, for yersel, Mistress Kerr an yer gude man, for baith o ye had been kind to me. An I wis gey fond o yer wee laddie wha is my maister noo, and a gude ane like his faither.'

The trade was in part lawful, but there was another part of which he became aware and into which he was persuaded to sink his savings. Three men sailed between Holland and Leith from time to time with a good cargo of silk, tea and tobacco. These confederates had more than their share of cunning and ingenuity, indeed of imagination. Knowing the power and persistence of the legend of Major Weir's coach, they had arranged with an innkeeper to have a black coach made and to find black horses, and themselves made those contraptions of wickerwork and cord and the false heads. In this way they had driven safely through the streets, depositing their goods, selling them later at an excellent price.

Their chief hiding-place was up the stairs behind that door where Thomas Kerr had, in his panic, taken refuge and where he had been caught up and carried off. The man who spoke to him was an excellent actor and had truly put the fear of death upon him. They had got away safely. There had been a black humour for them, the lawbreakers, in hearing the agonized confession of this respectable citizen, nearly demented by fear.

Then they had returned in high self-confidence, and the tale of that evening and of their routing by those twelve good men and their allies has been told.

'Sae noo ye ken hoo it has fared wi me,' Wattie ended his

John Knox's house, High Street

narrative. 'I wis left ruined, a my money entrusted to thae rascals. An sae I cam hame and cam to a kind welcome and thankful I am to be here.'

Thomas Kerr had been in some danger, for the smugglers had at one moment thought of taking him back to Holland and selling him to the Dutch East India Company as a labourer, since he could imperil them by informing. Then something – a mixture of awareness of his helplessness, his apparently feeble mind, which would make him harmless, and a touch of cynical pity: he was not worth bothering about – had made them thrust him out onto the road where he might be found or might die of cold. Little did it matter to them. They had disappeared – Wattie had no wish to know where; their confederate innkeeper had no doubt disposed of the coach and horses.

Old Mrs Kerr sent Wattie to tell her son the whole story. He told it to Dickson, and it was spread about the guild and about that part of the town, to be told and retold in the ale-houses in the High Street. It lasted longer than the fine tea and tobacco, though not longer than the good silk gowns.

You may find a moral in the tale: Thomas's fearful drive had been a catharsis. The Greeks so often have a word for it.

Source
John J. Wilson, *Tales of the Borders*, vol. 5, p. 238

15   The Deacon

The old lady sat by the fire, reading her Bible. It was the Sabbath and she had sent her servant lass to the kirk. She had not gone herself for she had been ailing somewhat and the doctor had told her to stay at home.

The door opened and a man came in, quietly. He was rather slight of figure, dressed soberly in black, as was proper on the Sabbath, and wore a mask. Bowing politely to the old lady, he picked up the keys that lay on the table beside her, opened her desk and took out a bundle of notes, locked the desk, placed the keys again on her table, bowed once more, very respectfully, and went out. She sat amazed.

Surely that was Deacon Brodie, his very look and build! Yet how could it be? He should have been at the kirk. Had he a double?

A crony of the Deacon's had a similar shock. Although he had mentioned to Brodie that he would be leaving town for a few days, something prevented his journey and he stayed at home. In the middle of the night he was awakened by a slight noise in the room next to his bedroom. High on the wall was a small window. He climbed on a chair, looked through and saw his friend the Deacon, masked and cloaked but distinctly recognizable, opening a drawer in his desk. From amazement or discretion or a blend of both, he made no protest, took no action.

William Brodie was born in 1742 in a house in Brodie's Close in the Lawnmarket. Following his father's craft, he showed great skill as a cabinet-maker. He was Deacon of the Guild of Wrights (cabinet-makers) more than once, and a town councillor—all this by the time he was forty. He was unmarried and lived with his unmarried sister, who kept house, but he kept two mistresses by whom he had children. This might have been deplorable by the strict standards of the day, but it did not in itself account for the double life for which he has become notorious: that came from his craft both as a cabinet-maker and as a criminal – he was as crafty a criminal as ever stood in the dock.

For many years he got away with it and prospered. In the end he came to his doom not through sins of the flesh but through the root sin of pride; the Greeks have a word for it, 'hubris' – over-weening self-confidence. It pays to be canny, to know when and where to stop leading the double life.

The double life was not unknown to Edinburgh (as anywhere else) and if kept within bounds was not criminal. Robert Chambers records in his *Traditions of Edinburgh* that shops were closed at eight o'clock, and at that time the Town Guard sounded the local form of the curfew, beating a drum 'as a signal for the warning from upper windows of *gardy-loo*.' Sir Walter Scott said that this '. . . was sometimes like the cry of the water-kelpie, rather the elegy than the warning of the over-whelmed passenger.' Chambers continues: 'It was in the evening of course that the tavern debaucheries assumed their proper character of unpalliated fierceness and destructive duration.'

A good deal could be packed into the two hours between eight and ten o'clock when some douce citizens took themselves home, more or less sober. Others, by no means douce, lingered. The Deacon was one of those. He belonged to one of the most notable taverns or clubs, the Cape, celebrated by that poet laureate of revelry Robert Fergusson.

> Now, some to porter, some to punch –
> Retire; while noisy ten-hours drum
> Some to their wife – and some to their wench, –
> Garr a' your trades gane danderin* home.
> Now, mony a club, jocose and free,
> Gie a to merriment and glee:
> Wi' sang, and gless, they fley the pow'r
> O' Care, that wad harass the hour:
> But chief, O Cape! we crave thy aid,
> To get our cares and poortith* laid.

Membership of the Cape was not held heavily against the Deacon any more than his illegitimate offspring by two mistresses. But his double life did not stop there.

Ironically, his skill as a craftsman helped to bring him down. A

Deacon Brodie

deft man with his hands, he found it easy to make keys —
duplicates, very useful for breaking and entering quietly. There
was a rumour, heard by William Creech the bookseller, that
Brodie had contrived the escape from the Tolbooth of a youth
about to be hanged for murder. The jailers were well soused with
drink, someone had a duplicate key, and the murderer was
brought out and hidden in Greyfriars Kirkyard, in the tomb of
Sir George Mackenzie, 'Bluidy Mackenzie', persecutor of the
Covenanters, whose ghost was said to haunt the place of his
burial.

Brodie's chosen 'gang' included Andrew Ainslie, a shoemaker,
George Smith, a grocer, and his wife, who had a shop in the
Cowgate, John Brown, alias Humphrey Moore, and one Clark,
who kept a tavern which was the favourite meeting place of the
gang. Brown/Moore was an especially useful member, for he had
a friend called Murray or Tasker who kept an inn, the Bird in
Hand at Chesterfield, where they stored their loot.

Breaking and entering continued in a most professional way,
with the Deacon's skill as a key-maker proving most useful. In
1786 the premises of Johnston & Smith, bankers, in the Royal
Exchange, were entered and banknotes to the value of £800
stolen.

The next raid was in Parliament Close (under the very shadow
of the law) on the shop of James Wemyss, jeweller, with a haul of
gold and diamond rings, brooches and earrings, and a quantity
of silver spoons. Then another jeweller's, Messrs Bruce in New
Bridge Street which led to the New Town, was burgled to a
considerable extent. There was a rumour of a masked figure
having been seen.

In the following year a grocer in Leith was robbed of three
hundredweight of fine tea, which at that time was a costly
luxury. And then the most spectacular and daring lifting of all:
the theft of the old and beautiful silver mace of the university, a
treasure which could not be replaced. A silk merchant was the
next victim — Messrs Inglis & Horner in the High Street: they
lost £500 worth of fine silk, satin and cambric. (John Gibson, the
Deacon's modern biographer, has suggested multiplying every
sum of money by twelve to give today's value.)

A reward was offered for any information but none was
forthcoming. The Lord Advocate, Ilay Campbell of Succoth,

communicated with London, and a free pardon was promised to any accomplice who would turn King's Evidence. The bad work continued.

Smith was as deft in the making of counterfeit keys as the Deacon himself. He copied those of another jeweller and gold-smith, Japp, having abstracted the owner's set which hung just inside the door. One of the gang, Brown, an acquaintance of Japp, called with a bottle and held him in talk, while Brodie, Ainslie and Smith collected their loot of gold and jewellery and a miniature in a frame backed with gold. Smith went secretly by night to the King's Park and hid part of their treasure under a stone, along with the forged key.

Then came the catastrophe through hubris, through treachery and through the affection of a faithful dog.

The Deacon led his followers into the most daring attack of all: on the General Excise Office in Chessel's Court. He had called there more than once, on apparently lawful business, made a careful survey, found that the key of the outer door hung just inside, taken it down and made an impression in putty. From this he made a duplicate.

Continuing his double part, he dined at home with his sister who kept house for him and with their married sister and her husband, Matthew Sheriff.

After dinner the two men went to a tavern but not for late or riotous drinking. The Deacon came home sober, went to his room and dressed for his part in the night's performance, in a dark suit and top-coat, cocked hat, black mask and wig; in his pockets he carried pistols and a dark lantern. He went to Smith's house to meet his fellow-performers: Brown, Ainslie and Smith, who found him very cheerful – to the point of hilarity – and confident.

They were well equipped with tools, including the coulter from a plough stolen from a field near the King's Park. Their separate parts in the performance were allocated: Ainslie to keep watch outside, Brodie inside, in the hall; Smith and Brown to raid the office itself and take the plunder. If a watchman approached, Ainslie would give one whistle, or three whistles if there were more than one watchman. Brodie would then warn Smith and Brown; Ainslie would go to a back window and help their escape. Stage, costumes, parts were all in order. A theatre manager could hardly have done better, but the performance was a crashing failure.

Smith and Brown found only £16 in the office instead of the vast sum they expected. As they searched frantically, they heard the front door open but took it for granted that Brodie would still be on guard. As the door shut with a bang, they ran into the hall. The guardian Deacon had vanished. The pair fled, leaving behind them the coulter and other equipment. Ainslie had already escaped.

All this was set off by the return of James Bonar, Deputy Solicitor of Excise, to collect some papers he had left in his room. Finding the door open, he assumed that one of the clerks had gone in. In the dimness he did not notice Brodie, did not hear him slip out. He collected his papers and departed.

Brodie went home, changed his suit and proceeded to the house of one of his mistresses, Jean Watt, with whom he spent the night. When the gang met next morning, he tried to laugh off his desertion, but this was not well received. Brown meanwhile went to the Sheriff-Clerk's office and laid information against Smith and Ainslie, though not against Brodie. He told it to an official, Middleton, who took him to the Procurator-Fiscal. Then he led the latter and Middleton to the hiding-place on Salisbury Crags where Smith had hidden his forged keys. Meanwhile Smith and Brown had their share of the £16, and with his, Smith bought a ticket for his wife on the coach to Newcastle, paying with a £5 note from the loot. But there was no escape. The Smiths and Ainslie were arrested. Though Mrs Smith was later released, the two men were lodged in the Tolbooth. Having handed over the forged keys, Brown was taken by Middleton on the coach to Chesterfield to recover the treasure left at the Bird in Hand.

Then comes the too-faithful dog. He had been with his master, Smith, when he hid the keys and when he stole the coulter. At their first interrogation by the sheriff, Smith and Ainslie were confronted by the ploughman John Kinnear whose coulter had been stolen. He had had only a glimpse of them and could not swear to their identity. At that moment the faithful dog ran into the office, leapt up at Smith, licked him affectionately and was, no doubt, cursed.

The wily Deacon did not appear. He had fled to England, on

the Sabbath, when all decent folk were at kirk. On Monday Smith heard of this defection and made a full confession, implicating the Deacon, giving full details of all the crimes.

There was then no Scotland Yard or CID, but there were King's Messengers. The King's Messenger in Edinburgh, Williamson, was sent off on the track of the Deacon. He picked up and followed several clues leading south to the Channel Ports but there the trail seemed to end.

Then came the dramatic entry of John Geddes, tobacconist in Mid Calder. He went to that most eminent of advocates Henry Erskine, who had been engaged by Brodie's family and friends as defence counsel in the case of a capture and trial. Geddes had a tale of Stevensonian quality.

He and his wife had been in London and were returning to Scotland by sea, in the *Endeavour* which belonged to the Carron Iron Company. While they lay one night at Gravesend, the captain, who had gone ashore, came back with another passenger, who gave his name as Dixon; he wore a shabby greatcoat, and he looked ill. The *Endeavour* sailed but ran aground at Tilbury and was held up for ten days. Geddes and his wife tried to make friends with Dixon but he was very aloof, besides suffering from a sore throat which made him only half-articulate. At last the *Endeavour* set sail – but not, as the Geddeses expected, for Leith – at least not at first.

When Dixon had come aboard, he had been accompanied by two officials of the Carron Iron Company. Now he produced a sealed letter from them instructing the captain to sail first for the Low Countries. There he disembarked at Ostend, after giving the deeply interested John Geddes a packet of letters to deliver on reaching home. When at last the *Endeavour* sailed to Leith and the travellers arrived home, Geddes opened and read the letters. He took them at once to Henry Erskine, hoping no doubt for a reward. After one glance, Erskine took them to the sheriff.

One, headed Flushing, 8 April 1788, was addressed to the Deacon's brother-in-law Matthew Sheriff; this was not a confession but a very business-like letter which might have been written by one going abroad on lawful affairs. He was going to Ostend and to Bruges. Would Matthew send him various tools: rule, quadrant and measuring rod, care of a clergyman in New

York, the Reverend Mr Mason. Apparently that was the Deacon's next port of call. Another cleric, in Edinburgh, the Reverend Mr Nairn, was, along with Matthew, in charge of the Brodie finances. The Deacon would be glad to hear from them, and from his sisters.

Other two letters were addressed, respectively, to Henderson, owner of stables in the Grassmarket and of the Cockpit which had been one of the Deacon's haunts, and to Ann Grant, his other mistress. The first told of his escape to London, to the house of an old female friend, then to Holland; the second expressed his paternal concern for his three children by Ann. The Deacon was undoubtedly a family man. 'They will miss me more than any other in Scotland. May God in His infinite goodness stir up some friendly aid for their support, for it is not in my power at present to give them the smallest assistance. Yet I think they will not absolutely starve in a Christian land where their father once had friends, and who was always liberal to the distressed.' Perhaps he was. The youngest child Jean should be sent to friends in Aberdeen to whom he would order a yearly payment of £6 to be made; her elder sister, Cecil (named after his mother), was to be apprenticed to a milliner and should also be taught writing and arithmetic. Perhaps a kind friend would take care of her: 'She is a fine sensible girl, considering the little chance she has had for improvement.'

The folly of these letters is almost incredible, but such folly is the sequel to hubris, as many a detective has declared and has proved. (The Deacon is among the first ancestors of the villain in the detective story.)

The law took immediate action. Already there had been too much delay. The Lord Advocate appealed to the Secretary of State, who wrote to the British Consul in Ostend, who spoke to one John Daly, giving him a description of 'Mr Dixon'. Daly remembered seeing this gentleman at the house of a vintner in Ostend, who confirmed this recollection. The net drew closer. A Public Office clerk, Groves, accompanied by a Bow Street Runner, was sent from London to Amsterdam, where a series of clues had led. There they found and arrested the Deacon and brought him under close guard to London and thence to Edinburgh.

*

The trial began in August, with Lord Justice Clerk Braxfield as presiding judge, accompanied on the bench by Lords Hailes, Swinton, Stonefield and Eskgrove. The Deacon's vanity may have been gratified by the sight of that most distinguished quintet, especially by Braxfield, one of the greatest characters of his time. His colleague Smith appeared with him in the dock. Brodie's Counsel was Henry Erskine, with Alexander White and Charles Hay as juniors; Smith's was John Clerk with Robert Hamilton. For the Crown appeared Robert Dundas, Solicitor General, and Ilay Campbell, Lord Advocate. It would be difficult to find a more distinguished company.

In the cultured eighteenth century the people of Edinburgh frequented the theatre and knew some great actors, but never had there been a greater melodrama than this, and it was set in Parliament House.

The double life of the Deacon was revealed, detail by detail. The end was inevitable. Brodie and Smith were found guilty and condemned to death by hanging. Murder was then by no means the only capital crime, and Braxfield pronounced doom. He has been held in reprobation for his cruelty on the bench, for his heartless mockery of the condemned, but at this trial he appears as a grave judge and not without compassion. It may indeed be said to be his greatest moment. He addressed the condemned men:

> I wish I could be of any use to you in your melancholy situation. To one of you it is altogether useless for me to offer any advice. You, William Brodie, from your education and habits of life cannot but know everything suited to your present condition which I could suggest to you.
>
> It is much to be lamented that those vices which are called gentlemanly vices, are so favourably looked upon in this present age. They have been the source of your ruin; and whatever may be thought of them, they are such as assuredly lead to ruin. I hope you will improve the short time which you have now to live by reflecting upon your past conduct, and endeavouring to procure, by sincere repentance forgiveness for your many crimes. God always listens to those who seek him with sincerity.

The prisoners were removed to the Tolbooth. According to William Creech, bookseller, who had been on the jury and was the Deacon's first biographer, they were '. . . chained by one leg to a bar of iron alongside of which they may walk, and their bed is made up by the side of it. Mr Brodie was allowed a longer chain than usual, a table and a chair, with pen, ink and paper.'

No visitors were admitted, for fear that one might smuggle in some poison to give him a quick exit. But Brodie declared he had no such intention. On the eve of execution he became somewhat agitated and said to Smith: 'Do you know what noise that is . . . it is the drawing out of the fatal beam on which you and I must suffer tomorrow.' The Deacon of Wrights had helped to design the new gallows (as Dr Guillotine had designed the instrument that would decapitate himself).

On the day of execution, 1 October, Brodie dressed himself and had his hair 'full dressed and powdered. Soon after a clergyman entered and offered to pray with him. He desired it might be as short as possible.'

At two o'clock in the afternoon the Town Guard surrounded the scaffold. Their Captain informed the magistrates waiting in the Council Chamber, who then came in solemn procession, robed, wearing white gloves and carrying white staves. They were followed by clergy in gown and bands. The prisoners were brought out, Brodie dressed in black, Smith in a white suit trimmed with black. 'They were assisted in their devotions by the Reverend Mr Hardie, one of the ministers of the city, the Reverend Mr Skeeve of the Episcopal, and Mr Hall of the Burgher persuasion. They spent some time in prayer, with seeming fervency. Brodie knelt, laying a handkerchief under his knees.'

When he first saw the crowd and the dreadful apparatus Brodie said. 'This is awful.' Then he spoke to an acquaintance among the spectators, saying that he was glad to see him. 'The gentleman answered he was sorry to see Mr Brodie in that situation, Brodie replied, "It is *fortune de la guerre.*"'

Smith was the first to be hanged, then Brodie, a dense crowd looking on. Creech reported that he

. . . deliberately untied his cravat, buttoned up his waistcoat and coat, and helped the executioner to fix the rope; then, pulling the night-cap over his face he folded his arms, and placed himself in an attitude expressive of firmness and resolution. Smith who had been in fervent prayer, soon after the adjustment of the halters, let fall a handkerchief as a signal, and a few minutes before three the platform dropt, and they were launched into eternity. Thus ended the life of William Brodie and of George Smith.'

Almost at once the legend was born that the Deacon had not died, that he had worn a steel collar beneath his neckcloth, that the hangman had been bribed, that a French doctor had been engaged to revive him after he was cut down and that he had been resuscitated and somehow carried off, eventually to escape to France, where he was sometimes later seen in Paris. Almost credible but not factual. The Deacon was dead, his neck broken, and he was buried in the kirkyard near George Square and Buccleuch Place.

Brodie died in body, but he lived and still lives in literature, in Creech's narrative and in the portrait, in both word and line, by John Kay, who also lived a double life – but in a most commendable manner. Kay was a barber and also an artist. He had a miserable childhood, having been given by his widowed mother into the charge of cousins who rivalled Dickens' Murdstones in cruelty. He was aware at an early age of his talent for drawing but was thrust into apprenticeship to a barber. In those days barbers were also surgeons, to some extent, adept in blood-letting at least. Young John served six years as apprentice, seven as journeyman, then became a Freeman of the Society of Surgeon-Barbers and prospered in his calling. His customers included many of the nobility and gentry, some eminent lawyers, Braxfield among them. In time he was able to retire and concentrate on his work as etcher and portraitist.

Kay's portraits are of unique strength and vividness and are matched by brief biographies. Of Brodie he wrote: 'From the masterly manner in which he accomplished his escape, baffled all pursuit for a time. . . . But for Brodie's own imprudence, impelled apparently by a sort of fatuity . . . there was every chance of his finally escaping.' He tells the story of the letters entrusted to Geddes: 'These letters, as he might well have expected, were the means of his discovery.'

Fatuity is a passable translation of hubris.

Kay also wrote of Brodie's 'Macheath-like boldness' and levity, a comparison which is inevitable and recurring. Indeed the Deacon would be a good subject for melodramatic opera. (R. L. Stevenson and W. E. Henley did write a play about him, but it was not a success.)

Kay made two etchings of Brodie, which well illustrate his double life. In one he is elegantly dressed, holding his cocked hat and a cane, with the tools of his craft on a table beside him; in the other he is accompanied by Smith and a fighting cock.

Brodie's most famous revival came through Stevenson. The Deacon begat Jekyll and Hyde, just as his judge, Braxfield, begat Weir of Hermiston. Stevenson wrote in *Edinburgh: Picturesque Notes*: 'A great man in his day was the Deacon; well seen in good society, crafty with his hands as a cabinetmaker, and one who could sing a song with taste. Many a citizen was proud to welcome the Deacon to supper and dismissed him with regret at a timeous hour, who would have been vastly disconcerted had he known how soon, and in what guise, the visitor returned.'

The Deacon was far from estimable. Though he was not violent he might have been ruthless, had his career continued, but he was not, like Edward Hyde, utterly evil and diabolical. (That character's remoter ancestor is Major Weir, Angelical Thomas.) The Deacon wore a dark cloak and a mask, but he was still himself underneath. The old lady to whom he bowed, after abstracting her money, said to herself, 'Surely that is Deacon Brodie,' but Dr Lanyon, the first to see Jekyll transformed into Hyde is shattered. The Deacon drank no evil drug, but Jekyll, as he confesses, '. . . had but to drink the cup, to doff at once the body of the noted professor, and to assume, like a thick cloak, that of Edward Hyde. . . . I was the first that could thus plod in the public eye with a load of genial respectability, and in a moment, like a schoolboy, strip off these lendings and spring headlong into the sea of liberty.' Again the fatal, primal sin brings destruction. Hyde thrusts out Jekyll, and Hyde is wholly evil. 'That child of Hell had nothing human; nothing lived in him but fear and hatred.' So he joins Major Weir.

The theme of the double life continues to fascinate story-tellers. Moray Mclaren used it in his novel about a judge whose disreputable nights were spent in the most sordid region of

Edinburgh, not far removed in space from the Parliament House of his professional duties and dignity, who murdered his mistress and in the end made his tragic exit. The legend, in one form or other, is part of the tradition of Edinburgh.

Sources
R. L. Stevenson, *Edinburgh: Picturesque Notes*
R. L. Stevenson and W. E. Henley, *Deacon Brodie, a play*
J. Kay, *Original Portraits*
John Gibson, *Deacon Brodie, Father to Jekyll and Hyde*

16   The Noose for Some

Two men were sentenced to be hanged, but because of a legal quirk one was released. His name was Elliott. There was no such remission for the other criminal, and on the morning of his execution a huge crowd gathered in the Lawnmarket to enjoy the spectacle.

Lord Medwyn, judge of the High Court, found himself by mischance among them. He could not reach Parliament Hall; the best he could do was to make his way to the upper end of the street, whence he looked gravely on. A man came towards him, not seeing him, running in agitation, and stood to watch the last act with eyes straining in torment.

The judge recognized him. It was Elliott, drawn to this act in horror, a spectator where he might have been one of the two actors.

Lord Medwyn told this to Henry Cockburn, his fellow judge, and Cockburn reflected.

It was a strange feeling that forced him there, but not incomprehensible.

Was Elliott guilty as his fellow? It is a tale that Scott should have told.

Duality lies deep, and evil may have charm of look and manner. Lord Cockburn knew this. He had one client, David Haggart, a murderer, who had killed his jailer in the prison in Dumfries. With all his legal detachment Cockburn was aware of the young man's charm. He was handsome, gentle in manner, apparently most amiable, '. . . but there never was a riper scoundrel – a most perfect miscreant in all the darker walks of crime. Nevertheless his youth (about twenty-five) and apparent gentleness, joined to an open confession of sins, procured him considerable commiseration particularly among the pious and the female.' (One can hear the whispers in court: 'Aw, the puir bonny laddie.')

But piety and sentimentality do not always (if ever) commend

Old Town from Princes Street

their subject to the bench; both may be perverted. Haggart was condemned to be hanged.

During his last days he dictated his memoirs and confession, and some poems. The manuscript he presented to Cockburn in acknowledgement of the effort he had made as defence counsel to win a reprieve. Cockburn was unmoved. The confessions and the whole book were a tissue of absolute lies. They were not an attempt at self-exculpation. They were an *apologia pro vita sua* of a perverted kind. Haggart wanted to '. . . appear a greater villain than he really was. Having taken to the profession of crime he wished to be at the head of it. He wanted to die a great man.' So he imagined and described crimes he had not committed. This was no purging of the soul by confession: he was proud of his evil-doing and would make it even blacker than it was.

'A strange pride, yet not without precedent, and in nobler walks of criminal ambition.' Writing that, what or whom did Lord Cockburn have in mind?

Cockburn records a tragic story of a murderess for whom he felt compassion, a Mrs Mackinnon. She had fallen pitifully, but she was not evil. 'A strong and lofty generosity, by which she had

*The new Bridewell, Salisbury Crags and Arthur's Seat
from Calton Hill*

been distinguished before she fell, neither the corruptions nor the habits of her subsequent life could extinguish.'

Mrs Mackinnon kept a brothel, and one night she stabbed to death, with a knife, a man who had started a brawl. For this she was tried and condemned. Had some circumstances which transpired later been known at her trial, the sentence might have been not for murder but for culpable homicide. Lord Jeffrey might well have prevailed on the jury to return that verdict. But those facts were not known until after her conviction. 'In law it was a murder and she was executed. So she died gracefully and bravely; and her last moment was marked by a proceeding so singular, that it is on its account that I mention the case.' There is, indeed, a ballad quality about it.

In her youth Mrs Mackinnon had been in love with an English Jew, and the love had endured. Now she sent him a message begging him to visit her in her cell. When he came, she took an orange which she had and cut it in half, giving one of the portions to him. Let him come to her execution and stand where they could see each other. She would put her half orange to her lips and let him do the same in token of faith and farewell.

It happened as she desired. He stood well within sight. She put half the orange to her lips, he made the same gesture of farewell.

'She saw her only earthly friend, and making the sign died, cheered by his affection.'

A true ballad ending – if only that had been the end. But Cockburn, the man of law, continues: 'Here the anecdote should have ended, and if it had been an invention it would have ended here. But how Nature's wonders exceed those of art.' The poor woman left all her money, £4–5,000 to this beloved friend. 'He took the legacy but refused to pay the costs of her defence, which her agent only screwed out of him by an action.'

Source
Henry Cockburn, *Journal*

17 Lord Monboddo – The Monkey o Jude

'He looked rather like an old stuffed monkey dressed in a judge's robes than anything else.' So Robert Chambers has described one of the most eminent scholars and judges of eighteenth-century Edinburgh – and that is to be of exalted rank. He was James Burnett, raised to the bench as Lord Monboddo, and he was a legend in his long lifetime (he was born in 1714 and died in 1799).

Burnett was of the landed gentry; he studied at Aberdeen and Edinburgh Universities, then proceeded to Holland, to Groningen, to concentrate on law. His return to Edinburgh was on the night of the Porteous Riots, when the mob dragged that wretched criminal from prison and hanged him. Young Burnett was mistaken, for the leader of the riot and came near to be being apprehended. This unusual prelude to a distinguished career at bar and bench is in keeping with his legend.

Burnett qualified as advocate in 1737 and was raised to the bench thirty years later. He married a beautiful wife who gave him one son and two daughters. The boy died young; one daughter married; the other, Elizabeth, who became a legend for her beauty, was unmarried and was her father's hostess. They lived in St John Street – '. . . that eccentric genius, Lord Monboddo, whose supper-parties, conducted in classic taste, frequented by the *literati*, and for a time presided over by an angel in form of a daughter . . .' – again to quote Robert Chambers – but for a time only, because this lovely girl (whom Burns, who met her once, declared to be the most heavenly of the Creator's works) had inherited her mother's delicacy with her beauty. She died of tuberculosis at twenty-five.

'Cover her face; mine eyes dazzle; she died young' might have been written of her. When she died, Burnett's son-in-law covered her portrait to spare her father a poignant reminder.

'Quite right. Quite right,' said Burnett, Lord Monboddo. 'Let us now go on with Herodotus.'

Catullus spoke that saddest line in poetry, '*Atque in*

Contemplation: Lord Monboddo

perpetuum frater, ave atque vale,' in hopeless grief. Monboddo may have recalled it with fortitude, in final dismissal.

What Burnett lacked in looks, he made up in brilliance of mind: a first-class scholar, especially in philosophy and the classics (he was as much at ease in Latin and Greek as in English, fluent in their use as well as steeped in their literature) and a most distinguished lawyer. He added to those gifts the spice and zest of eccentricity. This 'monkey-judge' believed in man's kinship with monkeys and that babies were born with tails which were nipped off by the midwife.

His suppers were given in the ancient mode of Greece and Rome, the wine bottles wreathed in flowers. Every night he had a bath (that alone an eccentricity at the time) with water impregnated with a blend of olive oil, rose water, Venice soap, a saline and some aromatic spirit which he believed to be that, or like that, used by the Romans in their unguents.

In religion Burnett was of the old Stoic fortitude and reticence. Whatever grief he felt for his wife, son and daughter, so early departed, he gave no sign. He was austere in habit, apart from his delight in rare food and wines and in fragrant hot baths. He would not drive in a carriage, because the Greeks and Romans had no such vehicle, but rode his horse not only on short journeys but to London and back every year. That would appear to have done *him* no ill, but for his fragile and docile daughter it was fatal. She was not allowed even a sedan-chair to carry her to and from concerts and assemblies. On a day of atrocious cold a rider, sitting face to his horse's tail, unable to face the bitter blast, met the only other travellers on the road — Monboddo and his daughter riding their horses.

Boswell met Monboddo and dined with him and with the Gaelic scholar the Reverend Dr Macqueen of Skye, in 1777. He wrote to Dr Johnson: 'They joined in controverting your proposition that the Gaelic of the Highlands and Isles of Scotland was not written till of late.' Dr Johnson rose to the bait, bringing the monkey tails with him: 'That Lord Monboddo and Mr Macqueen should controvert a proposition contrary to the imaginary interest of literary or national prejudice, might easily be imagined; but of a standing fact there ought to be no controversy. If there are men with tails, catch a Homo Caudatus; if there was writing of old in the Highlands or Hebrides, in the Erse language produce the manuscripts.'

Monboddo considered marrying again, and on one of his visits to London proposed to Mrs Garrick, widow of the great actor. The lady refused him.

During another visit to London he was given a seat in the court of the King's Bench. There was a sudden alarm that the roof was falling, and judge, barristers, witnesses and all rushed out.

The County Hall and Advocate's Library

Monboddo sat calmly where he was. Being somewhat deaf, he did not hear the rumour; the stampede he took to be one of those old English customs, part of a ceremony in which he, as a stranger, admitted only by courtesy, had no part.

He was one of the judges who heard and pronounced on the Douglas Cause which divided their lordships evenly, for and against the Douglases versus the Hamiltons, until the Lord President gave his casting vote. But of this more will be told.

Monboddo's last ride ended at Dunbar and in defeat. He was too ill and weak to continue, and take a chaise. 'I find I am eighty-four,' he said. A few days later he was dead.

He lives among the immortals of Parliament House. In a better world than this, he may have met Charles Darwin.

For our further delight Monboddo has been portrayed both in word and in line by John Kay in his *Original Portraits*. His portrait shows a face by no means monkey-like. It is called 'Contemplation' and presents Monboddo seated at his table with quill and notebook; he wears his wig and bands but not his robes. His look is at once contemplative, acute, benign and

Interior of the Advocate's Library

humorous. There is, perhaps, just a little of the monkey about his mouth. 'In a corner of the apartment hangs a picture in which his lordship's notion of tails is illustrated by a group of little fellows adorned with these appendages.'

Kay stresses Monboddo's amiability and generosity. He was far from wealthy as a laird, his estate bringing him not more than £300 a year, but he would not raise his rents 'nor dismiss a poor tenant.' 'It was his boast to have his lands more numerously peopled than any portion of equal extent in his neighbourhood.'

In the country during the vacation from the law courts he wore farmer's dress and '. . . lived on a footing of familiarity and kindness with his tenantry that greatly endeared him to them.'

In town his . . . private life was spent in the enjoyment of domestic felicity and in the practice of all the social virtues. Though his habits were rigidly temperate, there were few things he so much delighted in as the convivial society of his friends.'

Monboddo was a true lover of wine, caring for quality rather than quantity, honouring a noble vintage by restraint.

'He was a zealous patron of merit, and amongst those who experienced his friendship was the poet Burns.'

Finally Kay quotes an epitaph in verse written on him by James Tytler, an unfortunate son of genius who had experienced his benevolence.

> If wisdom, learning, worth demand a tear
> weep o'er the dust of great Monboddo here;
> A judge upright, to mercy still inclin'd
> A gen'rous friend, a father fond and kind.

Sources
Robert Chambers, *Traditions of Edinburgh*
J. Kay, *Original Portraits*

18   Piteous Love

It should have been, it could have been, a story of long and happy married love, true love, mutual love, with no shadow of infidelity. Yet this is a piteous tale, set in the eighteenth century.

The beginning was idyllic and of a pattern excellently common in Scotland. William Riddell was the only child of a shepherd on Tweedside and his wife. Mrs Riddell was a gentle and loving mother, caring for her husband and son, ready to listen, cherishing them both, and there was a strong and lovely bond of affection between them.

From the boy's earliest years, he and his father were companions. The shepherd was elderly to have so young a son; his had been a late marriage, but the years between them made no difference. David Riddell loved music, he played the flageolet and he taught young William to play the old country airs, the old psalm tunes. There were no love songs or dance tunes. These would not have fitted the gravity of David's character, but the psalm tunes were sweet, and they sang the praises of God and His creation. He was a patient and gentle teacher, and the boy was an apt pupil, with a sensitive ear and a sweet singing voice. Those days on the hill above the Tweed were idyllic.

Days at the parish school and winter evenings in the cottage were almost as good, for William was an eydent* and clever scholar. He loved to learn Latin, to read history; he was a born scholar who would, the dominie* predicted, go very far. His parents hoped and prayed that he would be a minister of the kirk.

In due time, indeed before the usual time, William was ready for college. His parents had saved all the money they could, and there was a bursary. Living would be frugal in lodgings in Edinburgh, but that was the pattern for most of the students. No one thought the less of a lad who had little to spend.

William fulfilled all the hopes of his parents, his schoolmaster and his professors. He took a high place in every class and after four years was capped Master of Arts. He came home for a

Trinity College Church

happy summer, most of it spent with his father on the hills. He continued to read and study, but he continued also to play the flageolet to the delight of his father. He was sturdy and healthy; there was no fear of his sinking into a decline as many a poor lad did.

The parting in the autumn at the beginning of the new college session was always sad. Old David took it calmly, looking forward to the student's return, happy in his success. The good mother too had this tranquillity. There was no anxiety about their son's health or about his behaviour. The only fear – it was the mother's more than the father's – was his emotional nature. William was too easily brought to tears, then quickly to laughter again; his grief at parting could be excessive. His mother warned him gently against this emotion.

There now came cause for grief. The dear wife and mother died. David took it bravely, for his faith was profound, but William was distraught. His uncontrolled grief distressed his father as it would have distressed his mother. Then the boy found comfort in writing of his sorrow. He wrote a beautiful and moving poem about his mother. The poem was published and it brought him much praise. The literary society of Edinburgh was fairly small and intimate, and the new name was noted, the new poet welcomed. It stimulated the young man to write more, both poetry and prose. He by no means neglected his studies; he was doing as well in the faculty of divinity as in that of arts, and his professors thought highly of him.

Now William begged his father to come and live with him. They could lodge together comfortably at a moderate cost. It would be good to come home to his father. Old David was deeply touched, but he would not come.

'Ye're a gude son and I'm proud that ye want me. But let me bide. I'd never tak kindly to the toun. It will aye* be the hills for me an the banks o Tweed and the glint o the streams. I'll manage fine by masel. I hae gude neighbours, and I think aye o yer mother. She's there in the land o the leal* and in the Lord's gude time I'll gae there to be with her. I still hae my health, I can help whiles wi the herdin. I'll aye be here to walcome ye, my son.'

So William continued his life of study and writing and pleasure, a good deal of all these elements, and they went well together.

He sometimes played the flageolet, though it was no longer the psalm tunes he played. This love of music quickened his talent for poetry and lightened his scholarship.

It has been said by the first narrator of this story that, 'The literary society of Edinburgh was by no means distinguished for its abstemiousness' – a masterpiece of understatement. It was, however, far from being of the ranting, roaring kind: it included some of the most respected and distinguished citizens, men of the clergy, men of letters and of the law (the latter notable for carrying their wine with dignity). Young Riddell was by no means ill seen. These revellers could emerge from their hilarious evenings into professional sobriety, decorum and expertise the next morning. (One of the best examples is Councillor Pleydell in Scott's *Guy Mannering*, an expert lawyer during the week and an hilarious reveller on Saturday night, but when Colonel Mannering and Dandie Dinmont desire his advice, he has only to wash hands and face in cold water and drink some tea to resume his legal dignity and wisdom.)

William was a comely youth, and more than one lady looked at him with favour. But he had lost his heart once and for all, and gained one in return. He fell in love, at one of the assemblies to which he was invited, with a bonny lass, who was as good as she was bonny and who returned his love with her whole heart. This girl, Ellen, was much above him in station – the daughter of a laird, his only child. Her father was displeased, even enraged. William's brilliance of mind, his popularity, his achievements and his promise of future and increasing success meant nothing to this man. To him, William was a peasant and the son of a peasant – on his own lands too – and not to be tolerated. But the lovers continued to meet, and they pledged their troth. Some of his professors may have looked grave, shaken a disapproving head, as William continued in his exuberance, his hilarity, but he gave no scandal, he never missed a class, he continued to distinguish himself in his studies.

There was a sudden misfortune for old David. His brother, who was in business, failed. He was heavily in debt, and in brotherly loyalty David made over his own savings to help pay the debts. Again William urged his father to come and live with him, but again the brave old man refused. He needed little, he was content. His presence might have controlled his son – but it

Ainslie Place

was doubtful. What did control him was his love for Ellen and hers for him. There was no wavering there, never then nor at any time a shadow of infidelity.

And so came his final tests, which he passed brilliantly, and he was licensed as a probationer and preacher. More than one of his professors came to visit him and his father in their cottage and were received by David with great dignity. The next step was ordination to the full ministry of the kirk. This came during the General Assembly, when David was an honoured guest. His heart was full of pride, of thankfulness to God, of tender memories of his wife. He met and loved Ellen, whom he cherished as a daughter.

Soon after William was appointed to a country parish not far from Edinburgh, he married Ellen, and for some time they lived in deep happiness. A son was born, and then at last David, the proud grandfather, consented to join his son and daughter in the manse. These were good years. Ellen was the kindest of daughters, William loved to recall his own boyhood, those days on the hillside above Tweed. They still played the flageolet, father and son; the children were lulled to sleep with sweet tunes.

William was a good minister; he cared for his people, and they were proud of him and of his fine sermons, eloquent, sound in teaching, poetic. He plunged deeply into theology and soared into poetry, and the Scots have a liking for both.

There was good company too in the neighbourhood. Men of culture were not lacking, and there was still good talk. There was also a good deal of drinking. This was not too severely condemned. It did not keep the minister from his studies, and strict sobriety was not prevalent. The old father was troubled, and so was Ellen. 'He's grand company,' said more than one of his congregation and neighbours. William began to suffer from the ancient sin of pride, of hubris as the Greeks called it, not conceit or vanity but an arrogant self-confidence. None could harm him.

His old father at last spoke to him very gravely, spoke of the grief it caused his wife, of the danger to their children. The son was contrite; he took the rebukes humbly and promised amendment. But it happened again. Late one night he was brought home helplessly drunk. Two of his parishioners were with him, kindly and discreet men, but it could not be kept secret. In deep distress old David left the manse and went back to Tweedside.

The shock of his departure sobered his son for a time, as the father had hoped. But it happened again. He was brought home in the early hours of the morning, not by one of his own people but by another minister, the pastor of the small Methodist congregation recently formed in the district. In his drunkenness William, being alone, had blundered to the door of this minister's house. The good man had opened to him and brought him home. He did not talk of it, but others did. The scandal spread. William's own people were ashamed of him, and some of his fellow ministers of the stricter sort were so scandalized that they brought the matter to the Presbytery.

The Presbytery were forced to take action. They decreed that William must make a public apology, from the pulpit, to his congregation. The penance was accepted. On that Sunday many of his faithful people, out of compassion, stayed at home. But others came, many from other kirks. This was too good to be missed.

Just before the service began, old David came in, supported by one of his neighbours. He was sadly feeble, bent, shrunken, his face deeply sad. He knelt in a pew at the back of the church. From the pulpit William read, with sorrowful dignity, his confession, his words of contrition. There were few who heard it without tears. There was a sudden groan. The old man slipped to the floor. He was gently lifted. His life was gone.

That was the beginning of a tragic end. Remorse and grief took the perverse form of increasing drunkenness. The scandal was intolerable. The Presbytery again took action and solemnly deposed the minister from his charge. He left the parish. For a time a good friend gave shelter to him and his wife and children. Then they drifted to Edinburgh, to poverty and degradation.

The tragedy has an epilogue, told by the original narrator. He was in Edinburgh one night, in Leith, coming home. A small crowd was gathered round the body of a woman. Helpless in drink, she had fallen beneath the wheels of a waggon. The narrator knelt and looked at the pitiful face. She opened her eyes, looked at him, and in his mind came a flash of recognition. This was Ellen Riddell. He had her carried to his house and laid her in bed. He tried to revive her, and there was a glimmer of recognition on her poor face. Then very faintly she murmured, 'My poor William. He was a social man.' And having spoken thus she died.

Source
John J. Wilson, *Tales of the Borders*

19 Young Love, Lost Love

This tale of lost love is not tragic; it is gently sad. The lover's heart may not have been broken but it was hurt and cracked; his love, unfulfilled, changed the life of the young Walter Scott.

He was to recover somewhat, to make a happy marriage, be a good husband and a loving and beloved father of whom his children stood in no awe whatever. But there remained this crack in the heart. He was one of the greatest storytellers – but not of love stories. His young lovers meet and after their share of difficulties and adventures, marry and are happy, but they are not ecstatic. Their creator guarded them and himself from passion.

The story began, most suitably, on a Sunday, outside the kirk of the Greyfriars which was attended by both families. As the kirk skailed,* rain was falling. Young Walter politely offered the shelter of his umbrella to a girl in a green silk mantle, and she was grateful. Both their parents were present and knew each other, if not intimately. She was Williamina Belsches, the only child of Sir John Belsches (later Stuart Belsches) of Fettercairn, and his wife Lady Jane. She was very young, only fifteen, and Walter was nineteen, but already walking the floor of Parliament Hall, where he would, in due course, proceed to advocate and later be Clerk to the Court (*sic sedebat* – thus he sat, as the carved letters announce on his statue).

Both families were of good name and standing: Scotts of the Border country, a farming family, Mrs Scott a sister of that most distinguished physician Dr Rutherford, who began the system of clinical medicine; the Belsches somewhat higher, country gentry, but not so exalted as to be removed from the Scotts.

The young folk met again from time to time, over the next year or two. Williamina 'came out' and was taken to the Assembly Balls which Walter attended, though he was, with his lame leg, no dancer. To his two most intimate friends, David Erskine and William Clerk of Eldin, he confided that, 'It was a proud night with me when I found that a pretty young woman could think it

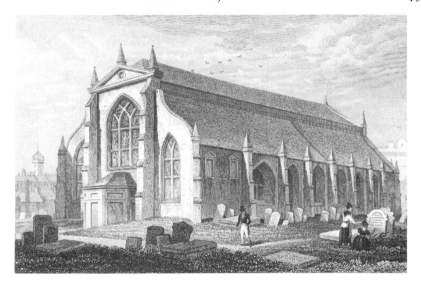

Greyfriars' Church

worth her while to sit and talk with me hour after hour, in a corner of the ballroom.'

Erskine wrote to him: 'Your Quixotism, dear Walter, was highly characteristic. From your description of the blooming fair as she appeared when she lowered her *manteau vert*, I am hopeful you have not dropped the acquaintance. At least I am certain that some of our more rakish friends would have been glad enough of the acquaintance.' Scott wrote to Will Clerk in 1792: 'I have no chance of seeing my *chère adorable* till winter, if then' – the Belsches summer was spent at Fettercairn.

Later he told his cousin William Scott that, 'The lady you allude to has been in town all this winter and going a good deal into public, which has not in the least altered the meekness of her disposition.' 'Meekness' may not sound the most attractive quality but it does convey gentleness, innocence, lack of pride and worthiness. Certainly young Scott, while proceeding steadily in his profession, a credit and comfort to his good parents, was not a brilliant match. He must have known that in his heart and been glad to see so little worldly vanity in the beloved. How did he stand between hope and anxiety? Did she appear to favour him?

Assembly Rooms, George Street

Long afterwards, forty years on, when Scott was dead, at the height of his fame, Clerk wrote to Scott's daughter Sophia:

> Your father's penchant for the lady began, I think in the year 1790. (Her mother, Lady Jane, was an acquaintance of his mother, which led to a visiting acquaintance.) It was a prodigious secret at first which I discovered by observing that he wore a sort of medallion in the style of Tassie's heads about his neck, which had been made for him by a Mons. Guildbert, a French artist, and shortly afterwards he told me all about it. He certainly was much attached to her.

Clerk's statement is the more convincing for its restraint and formality. With his own letter Clerk sent one which young Walter had written to him in those youthful years, in 1795 – a letter which is a key to the young lover's heart.

> It gave me the highest satisfaction to find that you have formed precisely the same opinion with me, both with regard to the interpretation of ......'s letter as highly flattering and favourable, and to the mode of conduct I ought to pursue – for after all, what she has pointed out is the most prudent line of

conduct for us both, at least till better days, which I think myself now entitled to suppose she as well as myself will look forward to with pleasure. If you were surprised at reading the important billet you may guess how agreeably I was so at receiving it, for I had, to anticipate disappointment struggled to suppress every rising gleam of hope and it would be very difficult to describe the mixed feeling her letter occasioned which, *entre nous*, terminated in a very hearty fit of crying. I read over her epistle about ten times a day, and always with new admiration of her generosity and candour – and as often take shame to myself for the mean suspicions which, after knowing her so long I could listen to, while endeavouring to guess how she would conduct herself. To tell you the truth I can not but confess that my *amour propre* which one would expect should have been exalted has suffered not a little upon this occasion through a sense of my own unworthiness.

This letter may be a key to open a secret drawer, but the drawer when opened holds no treasure. Williamina's to Walter is not there.

Walter's own letter to Will Clerk continues: 'I was always attentive, when consulting with you upon the subject of my declaration, rather to under- than to over-rate the extent of our intimacy. . . . Oh for November! Our meeting will be a little embarrassing. How will she look?'

There is hope in that letter, but the shadow of doubt lingers and it was to darken. There were other meetings, a visit to Fettercairn, other talks. Scott the young advocate went to Aberdeen on legal business; Scott the future antiquary visited Dunottar with the parish minister to see the digging of an ancient well; Scott the Border Minstrel collected some northern poems and ballads. Scott the lover was ardent and hopeful. But the end was near.

There was a rival suitor, and he won the lady. Scott was for a time bitter, but Williamina had not been treacherous, nor had she been worldly. The rival was wealthy and of high degree. Sir William Forbes of Pitsligo, came from an old family of Jacobite loyalty; he was a banker – and in Scott's day of distress was to be a good friend, but above all he was a good man, worthy to be loved, and Williamina probably accepted him out of love.

It left that crack in the heart, that reluctance to plunge into passion of which Scott in maturity was to write in a letter to Lady Abercorn:

I gained no advantage from three years of constancy except the said experience and some advantage to my conversation and manners. Mrs Scott's marriage and mine was of our own making, and proceeded from the most sincere affection on both sides which has rather increased than diminished during twelve years marriage. But it was something short of love in all its forms which, I suspect, people only feel once in their lives. Folk who have been nearly drowned in bathing rarely venture a second time out of their depths.

Scott's friends were dismayed by the news and felt something of his own shock. According to one account, he heard it first one evening when he was with some friends in a tavern. At another table someone announced cheerfully and casually that Miss Belsches was to marry young Forbes. Scott's glass broke in his hand.

From this shock came his poem 'The Violet,' in which there is a touch of bitterness.

> The violet in her greenwood bower
> Where birchen boughs with hazel mingle,
> May boast itself the fairest flower
> In glen or copse or forest dingle.
> Though fair her gems of azure hue
> Beneath the dewdrops weight reclining
> I've seen an eye of lovelier blue
> More sweet through wat'ry lustre shining
> The summer sun that dew shall dry
> Ere yet the day be past its morrow
> No longer in my false love's eye
> Remained the tear of parting sorrow.

But was she false? She was kind and gracious; she liked him very well, with an affection that probably came short of love such as he felt and desired. In another poem, found and given to us by Sir Herbert Grierson, he wrote:

By a thousand fond dreams my weak fancy betrayed
Believed thee for love and for constancy made
Believed that Indifference never could be
When gentle Compassion had pleaded for me.

He reproved himself for folly, almost presumption:

Oh fool to imagine such graces could be
By Nature formed only for love and for thee.

Then again reproach:

For grandeur for wealth your poor friend you resign
If Bliss they can give, oh, may it be thine.

But it was for much more true qualities that Williamina had resigned her poor friend. Sir William Forbes was a good man. who loved her dearly and whom, we may believe, she loved in return.

There was no betrayal, no acceptance of an unworthy lover – as Scott knew in his heart and would prove later. He loved so deeply that he could not guess or imagine that her love might be moderate: a kind affection, no passion; and he was over-sensitive about his comparative poverty – he had too little hope, too little faith in himself.

Unfriended by Fortune, untutored by Art,
I gave you my all when I gave you my heart.

How great a treasure that was, he was too modest to realize.

The heart did not break but it carried a wound until the end of his life. And he gave one of his most attractive heroes the heart's desire he had himself been denied: Alan Fairford in *Redgauntlet*.

That douce (or not so douce) young advocate falls in love with Lilias, the mysterious visitor come to consult his (decidedly douce) father. She is enchanting in her green mantle. Then there is the brief agony of thinking she may be Darsie's love, and soon the blessed relief – she is Darsie's sister and Alan is free, indeed encouraged, to woo and win her.

Alan is recognized by readers as the young Scott himself,

Abbotsford, home of Sir Walter Scott

Darsie, usually, as his friend Will Clerk. But a better reading is to see the young Scott in both. He was the most complex of characters: truly a lawyer, not forced into his profession, as well as a poet, a storyteller, an historian and antiquary. There was a Darsie as well as an Alan in him, and that is revealed by the story of his lost love as well as by his delight in valiant deeds.

The question lingers. Would he have been as happy as he had dreamed with Williamina – supposing she had returned his love in full measure? His marriage was happy, if short of rapture; it brought him his dearly loved and loving children, and one of the most moving passages in his journal is that which tells how sorely he missed his wife Charlotte when she died.

Sources
Adam Scott, *The Story of Sir Walter Scott's First Love*
H. J. C. Grierson, *The Story of Scott's Early Love*, Blackwood's
   Magazine, No. 241, Feb. 1937
Donald A. Low, *Scott's Lost Love*, Scots Magazine, Aug. 1971
Carola Oman, *The Wizard of the North*

20   The Nuns' Return

'Nothing of late has shocked some people in Edinburgh or entertained others more than the reappearance of a regular Catholic nunnery with its small chambers, its chapel and its Sisters of Charity. It has been built at Whitehouse, near Bruntsfield Links, from funds supplied by old Menzies of Pitfodels, a Catholic Aberdeenshire laird.'

So Henry Cockburn wrote in his journal on 15 March 1835. His account is commendably objective. Much of his journal deals with Church affairs, especially later with the Disruption of the Free Kirk from the Established and with the complication of Presbyterian sects.

Cockburn writes of the gradual growth of tolerance: 'The toleration of the Catholics by the people is one of the striking changes of our time. Since I was born their only chapel was destroyed by the mob (1780) and the secret feeling of most true Protestants for long after was that that was rather virtuous excess. After that, the true old historical hatred of them was aggravated because it was Catholics who made the French Revolution.' This would seem a distinctly unfair accusation. It was made also against the Radicals in politics. One of the most brilliant and agreeable ladies of eighteenth-century Edinburgh was Mrs Fletcher, who, with her husband, was suspected of sympathizing with the Revolution. It was solemnly declared and believed by some that the hens in her yard were decapitated by a miniature guillotine, as symbol and practice for human executions.

The mere approach to repeal of the penal laws against Catholics brought the Gordon Riots in London and in Edinburgh the burning of the chapel in Chalmers Close; one fervent Protestant would gladly have seen the burning of the bishop as well.

This bishop was one George Hay, born in 1729 of an old family with non-jurant and Jacobite sympathies. He was a student of medicine in Edinburgh under Dr John Rutherford, grandfather of Sir Walter Scott. When Prince Charles Edward appealed after Prestonpans for medical and surgical help for the wounded, young Hay volunteered. He went with the Jacobite army to Culloden, was there made prisoner and was taken to London. As a non-combatant, he suffered no more than imprisonment, and after his release he returned to Edinburgh and his medical training. Between release and return he had lived for a time with some kinsfolk in whose house he had found and read some works of Catholic theology and devotion. Their influence drew him to the old religion, and in 1748 he was received into the Catholic Church.

In Edinburgh Hay finished his studies and qualified as a member of the Royal Medical Society, but, as a Catholic, he was debarred from taking their diploma. For a time he kept a chemist's shop in the city, then he sailed as a ship's surgeon.

That voyage brought a second spiritual crisis and decision. Hay met the saintly Bishop Challoner, translator of the *The Imitation of Christ*, annotator of the Douai Bible, author of a spiritual classic, and under his influence Hay realized his own vocation to the priesthood. He left the ship, went to Rome, to the Scots College, and in due time was priested in 1758.

Returning to the Scots Mission, Hay was sent to the Catholic charge of Presholme, Banff. His medical training was not given up. He served people in body as well as in soul, vowing never to take a fee for any work of healing.

In 1769 he was consecrated Bishop, with the title *in partibus* of Daulie; the custom of the period when no English or Scottish diocese could be given to a Catholic. His actual region was the Lowland district, and it was then that he came to Edinburgh one day and to the burning chapel in Chalmers Close. He asked what had happened. No one recognized him as bishop for, in discretion, the Catholic clergy wore lay dress in public.

'Eh, Sir', said one fervent old wife, 'we are burning the Popish chapel, and we only wish we had the bishop to throw into the fire.'

From that digression we come back to the more tolerant decade of the 1830s – not, however, a complete tolerance. There was still a feeling that the Papists were favoured by the Whigs, and then: '. . . the atrocities produced by misgovernment in Ireland were uniformly ascribed to its religion. Even yet there are thousands of worthy people who not only retain all the horror of their ancestors against the professors of this creed but would like to see them still persecuted. But this weakness is abating.'

It was becoming necessary to accept Catholics, especially the poor. There were flocks of poor Irish workers especially in Glasgow and the west and, '. . . it was found absolutely indispensable to educate and civilise them'. This familiarized people with their chapels, their schools, and their openly associating; and admitted priests into measures of public charity.

Then came a snob reason for toleration. Exiled royalty has always had a certain appeal, and in 1830 the exiled French royal family came to Edinburgh and Holyrood, where they made '. . . the popish chapel near the east end of York Place a sort of fashionable Sunday resort.' Yet it was never a merely class or snob development. 'The whole country was overrun by Irish labourers, so that the Presbyterian population learned experimentally that a man might be a Catholic without having the passions or the visible horns of the devil. New chapels have arisen peacefully everywhere . . .' Except for an occasional outbreak by the Irish now and then, from 'their stronger taste for a fight, on both sides there was increasingly decent behaviour: 'The recent extinction of civil disability on account of their religion removed the legal encouragement of intolerance, and left common-sense some chance; and the mere habit of hating, and of thinking it a duty to act on this feeling, being superseded, Catholics and rational Protestants are more friendly than the different sects of Protestants are.' Sectarian disputes could be as bitter as family quarrels. Catholics being outside the Protestant, Presbyterian family were tolerated, even accepted with good humour.

So 'the nunnery has arisen undisturbed by violence.' There lingered, however, a shadow of superstitious dread: 'Many of the wrights and masons, particularly the old ones, feel uneasy at touching it, and often explain that they are mere workmen.'

The nuns returned, their pupils arrived. Convent and school were dedicated to St Margaret of Scotland. St Catherine was, no doubt, remembered and gave her blessing.

In 1850 the convent saw a dramatic spectacle. The old Catholics had never failed in worship but they had been, of necessity, very discreet. Now the spectacular devotion spread from France and Italy. The feast of Corpus Christi was

High School, Wynd

celebrated in the open, with a procession. To walk through the streets carrying the Sacred Heart, the Corpus Christi, would still have been dangerous, but to hold the celebration in the garden of the convent was entirely safe.

The procession emerged from the chapel, led by cross-bearers and acolytes, then came the pupils in white gowns and veils, then the clergy followed by the bishop walking front of the canopy held by the Brothers of Saint Vincent de Paul; beneath the canopy walked Bishop Carruthers carrying the Sacred Heart, Corpus Christi, the body of Christ.

Source
Henry Cockburn, *Journal* for 15 March 1835

21　The Doom of the Ogilvies

The Scots are a dramatic race, with a history full of tragedy and ironic comedy, yet not until the present century have there been many good Scots plays. In the eighteenth century, the age of enlightenment when the shadows of Calvinism receded, there was a decided interest in the theatre. Edinburgh saw Mrs Siddons (even the General Assembly on the Kirk was interrupted by the desire to attend her performances), and John Home presented his tragedy *Douglas*. But there was no flowering of drama by Scottish playwrights.

The nation's genius for tragedy, the sense of tears in human things, has been expressed in the ballads, most succinctly and poignantly, and for drama in the trials in Parliament House. That was the true popular theatre. The players were the judges, the advocates and the criminals (known as 'the panel' in Scots law). The audiences were largely made up of the populace, who were critical of the presentation of both defence and prosecution and of the final summing-up.

Scott knew this and in *The Heart of Midlothian* portrayed a typical follower of such drama in Mr Saddletree, who kept 'an excellent and highly esteemed shop for harness, saddles, etc,' whose prosperity depended less on himself than on his very capable wife. His own '. . . genius lay towards the weightier matter of the law, and he failed not to give frequent attendance upon the pleadings and arguments of the lawyers and judges in the neighbouring square, where, to say the truth, he was oftener found than would have been consistent with his own emolument . . .' – but for that good wife.

Mr Saddletree was a connoisseur, as were many fellow citizens. A murder trial brought a packed court (unless it was held *in camera*), with a mob outside and, if the verdict were guilty, round the scaffold.

The trial of Katharine Nairn (or Ogilvie) and her brother-in-law Patrick Ogilvie, for the double crime of incest and murder, had the duality of a ballad and of tragic drama – of a Greek tragedy of Aeschylean quality. From the beginning there is the sense of doom.

The story has been told briefly by Robert Chambers in *Traditions of Edinburgh*; it has also been told fully and in professional detail by the late William Roughead from 'the original record in the Books of Adjournal of the High Court Justiciary' and other documents made known to him. It has also been made into a novel, *The Laird*, by Winifred Duke (1925), which opens with the quotation of a ballad:

O whaur ha'e ye been, Lord Ronald, my son
   Mither, mak my bed sune
For I'm sick at the heart and I fain would lie doun.

O what will ye leave to your true love, Lord Ronald, my son?
   The tow and the halter for to hang on youn tree,
And let her hang there for the poisoning o me.

Katharine Nairn

The trial of Katharine Nairn (or Ogilvie) and her brother-in-law Patrick Ogilvie is one of the greatest tragic dramas ever produced at the High Court in Edinburgh. They had been brought there from the family estate, Eastmiln in Angus, by boat to Leith, thence to the city and the Tolbooth, where the mob was dense and ferocious, Edinburgh crowds not being known for their reticence.

The Aeschylean note is heard at once. The Ogilvies were a Jacobite family and paid for that loyalty. Thomas Ogilvie, the laird, was imprisoned in Edinburgh Castle. In 1751 he tried to escape over the wall, fell and broke his skull. He was survived by his wife Isobel, henceforth called, after the old Scots fashion, Lady Eastmiln, and also by a daughter and four sons. There had been five sons, but three years before, the eldest had gone mad and hanged himself. This end has more than a touch of the macabre: 'It is said that the place where he hang up himself was too low, and he came down and delved below his feet to make it proper for him.' A younger brother, William, '. . . went on board a Man of War as carpenter and was crushed to death twixt two Ships. Thomas and Patrick the Lieutenant how they made their Exit is well known.'

The way towards that exit is told here.

Thomas, the second son, succeeded to the estate; Patrick was a lieutenant in the 89th Regiment of Foot, serving in the East Indies; Alexander, the youngest, was a doctor living in Edinburgh. Their only sister Martha had married Andrew Stewart, a merchant in Alyth, regarded, perhaps, by the family as somewhat beneath them, but not too far, not nearly so far as Alexander's wife, the daughter of a street porter in Edinburgh; Alexander was promptly cut off.

Katharine was the younger daughter of the late Sir Thomas Nairn of Dunsinnan (Dunsinane, name of ill omen). In 1764 she came to stay with her sister Bethia, wife of another Angus laird, Spalding of Glenkiltry, a friend of Thomas Ogilvie – 'Eastmiln' to give him the usual lairdly name. She was nineteen, pretty, lively; he was forty in years but much older than that in temperament – a good deal of an invalid, a dwaibly body.* He fell in love at first sight, proposed and was accepted, against the wishes of Katharine's family, who were wise in this matter. The

ill-matched pair were married on 29 January 1765 and Eastmiln
brought his young bride to his own house.

The laird's house was far from ample – it was almost mean.
On one side of the door was the kitchen, above it the west
bedroom, that of the laird and his wife. On the other side was the
parlour and above that the east bedroom, with two beds.
Between the rooms was a large closet or storeroom. Two maids
shared a box bed in the kitchen; a third bedded down in the byre.
Every sound in the west bedroom was audible in the kitchen. A
close-packed dwelling with small place for quiet or secrecy.

When Patrick, the Lieutenant (sometimes unofficially pro-
moted and called Captain), came home from the East Indies, he
was broken in health but, unlike his brother, an interesting, even
an attractive invalid: handsome, musical (he played the violin),
susceptible. He was given the 'east bedroom.'

Then another occupant arrived, who was to prove the
catalyst: Anne Clark, a cousin of the family, sent by Alexander.
Her reputation was far beyond any doubt, as was revealed at the
trial, although how much Lady Eastmiln, the laird and Patrick
knew at this time can only be guessed.

Anne had lived with Alexander until he married. Before that
she had been a popular member of a 'noted bawdy house.' (This
was duly set forth at the trial.) Alexander sent her as agent to
work what ill she could, and she was not lacking in skill. He had
been shattered by Eastmiln's marriage to a healthy young
woman, for he had thought to succeed his brothers in the
inheritance. The laird was known to be in poor health; his
brother-in-law Andrew Stewart deponed at the trial that he had
heard his wife Martha say of her brother, '. . . he would not be a
long liver', and Katharine's brother-in-law, Spalding, told her
mother, Lady Nairn: 'Eastmiln was threatening a decay some
time ago, and I do not think him in a good way now.'

So there were three actors in a potential tragedy complicated
by Alexander's furious disappointment at the prospect of being
ousted from the succession – potential, even without the
interruption of that active and dexterous agent Anne Clark.

An excellent actor, she played the part of a kind young
kinswoman to old Lady Eastmiln, who appears to have liked her
and who probably did not know her past and her reputation.

Katharine and Patrick, if they were indeed lovers, were almost incredibly stupid, especially Katharine, if she were planning the murder by poisoning of her husband. It is known that the cleverest criminals, especially murderers, being filled with hubris among other sins, some time or other give themselves away, carelessly leave a clue. Katharine's sheer stupidity in this matter could almost be held as proof of her innocence – as William Roughead indicates.

Anne, that guardian of morality and the family honour, warned Katharine, told her that she had heard, from the stairs, and seen evidences of the highly improper relations between her and Patrick. She spoke gravely but was ignored.

Katharine was not reticent about her dislike of her ailing and no doubt querulous husband. She declared her intention of buying poison – either from a merchant in Perth or from a seedshop in Edinburgh. Anne pointed out the madness of such a plan and offered to procure a dose from Dr Alexander. This, however, she did not do. She told Lady Eastmiln of Katharine's wild talk, and the old lady warned her son against taking any food or drink from his wife's hand, telling him that Katharine had been 'troublesome.'

Suddenly a quarrel flared up between the brothers, about some money – a bond due to Patrick unpaid. He, by his own account, left the house vowing never to return. Anne's version was that Eastmiln had ordered him to go. Another violent quarrel followed between Eastmiln and Katharine, in their bedroom, every word excitingly audible to the maids in the kitchen beneath. Anne, sharing Lady Eastmiln's box bed in the parlour, had every opportunity to express her suspicions.

At the trial it was stated by one deponent, or witness, Elizabeth Sturrock, a maid in the house, that Mrs Katharine Ogilvie had sent her with a letter to the Lieutenant, who was staying with a friend, George Shaw, near Little Forter. He read the letter and bade the maid assure her mistress that all was well. There were other letters. Patrick moved to other friends' houses, then to Katharine's sister and brother-in-law, the Spaldings, at Glenkiltry.

The strangest and most unexpected letter of all was from his brother Eastmiln himself, carried by a neighbour, James Millam, while Patrick was still at Little Forter. This Eastmiln read to Millam. It was most conciliatory. He asked Patrick to return, telling him that he himself was going to Edinburgh for some weeks and that this would show his confidence in Katharine and Patrick, his rejection of the gossip and scandal about their relations. Patrick wrote a reply which he read to Millam, declining the invitation because of the rumours. When Millam brought that letter to the laird, he was told that it was addressed to Katharine, and to deliver it to her. There could hardly have been a more emphatic declaration of trust.

Patrick then rode, with a fellow officer, to Brechin, where he stayed for a night at the house of a vintner, Colin Smith. He then wrote to a friend, Dr Carnegie, inviting him to dinner. When the doctor arrived, Patrick told him that he was 'troubled with gripes' and asked for some laudanum; also for some arsenic with which to put down some troublesome dogs. The doctor provided both drugs and charged one shilling. This was on Friday 31 May. Having spent the weekend with his friend and fellow officer, Campbell, Patrick rode on Monday 3 June to the Stewarts at Alyth. (He rode one of his brother's horses.) Next morning the maid Elizabeth Sturrock brought another letter from Katharine and was given a reply.

That day Andrew Stewart (as he said at the trial) '. . . saw the Lieutenant working among some salts, at least, which appeared to the deponent to be salts, which were in a chest belonging to the Lieutenant.'

On the following day Stewart announced that he was riding to Eastmiln. At the trial he '. . . being purged of malice and partial counsel, sworn and interrogated, depones that upon the evening before Mr Ogilvie died, being a Wednesday, the deponent was at the house of Eastmiln, when, upon his coming into the house, Mr Ogilvie told him he had forbid his brother, the Captain [Patrick is given both this rank and that of Lieutenant by deponents] the house on account of suspicions he had that his wife was too much taken up with doing things for his brother the Captain, and not for himself.' This may seem to contradict that earlier letter bidding Patrick return. Had the laird been brooding over his wife's neglect? The tone is querulous rather than bitter or vengeful.

Andrew Stewart continued that, before he left for Eastmiln, Patrick gave him '. . . a small phial glass containing something liquid which he said was laudanum, and also a small paper

Waterloo Place, the National and Nelson's monuments and Calton Hill

packet which he said contained salts.' This to be given '. . . privately into Mrs Ogilivie's own hand [with a letter] sealed both with wax and a wafer.'

When he arrived at Eastmiln, Andrew Stewart 'was carried into a room where old Lady Eastmiln was' and where they were joined by Katharine and Anne Clark. Katharine asked him to come up with her to 'the easter room' where he gave her the phial, the packet and the letter. Later Anne Clark asked him what he had brought with him; he declared 'nothing' but 'upon Miss Clark's pressing him with great earnestness, he at last informed her of the particulars he had brought.' Miss Clark then said she feared that Mrs Ogilvie might poison her husband.

Both she and Lady Eastmiln urged the laird to take nothing from his wife's hand, by which Andrew Stewart was much displeased. At that time he had no suspicion of any such plan by Katharine. That night '. . . he heard Mrs Ogilvie say that she lived a most unhappy life with her husband; that she wished him dead, or if that could not be, she wished herself dead.'

At supper Eastmiln appeared in 'his ordinary state of health' but said that that afternoon he had 'swarfed, or fainted on the hill.' He did not appear at breakfast. His wife filled a bowl with tea, adding milk and sugar, and took it up to him. An hour and a half later they were told that he was suddenly taken very ill. Anne Clark ran upstairs and returned to report that 'Eastmiln had got a bad breakfast.' Andrew Stewart then went up and found him being violently sick and heard him say that 'all was wrong within; and that he had got what would do his turn.'

When he asked for drink, they offered him milk but he would have nothing but water. He complained that he was burning within. His demand for a doctor was at first refused by his wife who '. . . would not for any that a surgeon be called, as the consequence of this would be to give her a bad name from what Miss Clark had said of her' but she agreed to Andrew Stewart's suggestion of calling in Mr Meik in Alyth, a discreet man who 'would tell none but her what he thought of him' (of the laird). It would appear that old Lady Eastmiln had told Stewart that she had gone up to the bedroom door after the laird and that there was more kindness between them than usual. Katharine herself had been unwell: she had been 'blooded and was taking drugs.'

Elizabeth Sturrock deponed at the trial that late in the afternoon of that last day Anne Clark, 'who sat close by him', told her to go down and tell Mrs Ogilvie to come up and see her husband, who objected. 'No, no, I do not want her.' But the maid went down and, 'Mrs Ogilvie refused to come up, saying, she did not like to see dying people.'

Another maid in the house, Anne Sampson, deponed at the trial that she had brought the laird water in the bowl from which he had drunk that tea at breakfast, and he had cried, 'Damn that bowl for I have got my death in it already.' When his mother reproached him for having taken anything from his wife's hand, he moaned feebly: 'Oh, mother, mother, its too late to reproach me now for she forced it on me' and again 'My death's upon my wife and my brother, for surely he has connived with her in this.'

> Mither, mither, mak my bed sune,
> For I'm sick at heart and I fain wad lie doun.

To his friend and neighbour James Millam he said, 'I am gone, James, with no less than poison.'

This was 6 June. At midnight Eastmiln died. About two hours later Dr Meik arrived. He saw Katharine, who appeared to be in a proper and sufficient condition of grief. At the trial he said that she had '. . . desired the deponent that, whatever he might think he discovered to be the cause of her husband's death, that he would conceal it from the world . . . There was nobody else present with the deponent and the pannel.' An excellent opening to a detective novel.

On leaving the house the doctor met Patrick, and together they went up to the death-room. Patrick also appeared to be in a state of grief.

The funeral was arranged for 11 June. That morning, early, Alexander arrived from Edinburgh and forbade it. The pitiful body was carried to an outhouse. It must, by Alexander's demand, be examined for poison. Who put this suspicion, this demand, into his mind? Anne Clark was to swear upon oath that she had told no one of her own suspicions.

Katharine sent for him but he refused to see her or speak to her. This brought on a fit of crying, intensified by the news that the funeral was postponed. Alexander then sent to the Sheriff at Forfar a formal written accusation of his sister-in-law and his brother Patrick of having murdered the laird. On 12 June he summoned two doctors, besides Dr Meik: Dr Ramsay and Dr John Ogilvie, who later gave evidence at the trial.

On Friday the 14th the Sheriff Substitute of Forfar, Campbell, arrived at Eastmiln, interrogated Katharine and Patrick and took them back with him to Forfar where he committed them to jail. Four days later the Crown Agent, John Davidson, instructed Andrew Murison, Macer of Justiciary, to bring the prisoners, closely guarded, to Edinburgh. They were brought to Leith, where Katharine was in danger of being stoned by the mob, not only for her alleged crime but for her levity of conduct.

Meanwhile Sheriff Campbell of Forfar returned to Eastmiln, where Alexander had taken possession of everything, including Katharine's keys. He found two letters from her to Patrick; a third was later sent him by Alexander; this was unsigned, and whether or not it was genuine is open to doubt and debate. Anne Clark was certain that it was in Katharine's writing but some might think that Anne was not an impeccable witness.

On 5 August the trial began before the High Court. Sir Gilbert Elliot of Minto, Lord Justice Clerk, presided, accompanied on the bench by Lords Auchinleck (Boswell's father), Alemore (Pringle), Kames (Home), Pitfour (Ferguson) and Coalston (Brown).

For the Crown appeared Thomas Miller, Lord Advocate, James Montgomery, Solicitor General, and David Dalrymple. For the defence (for Katharine) Henry Dundas, later Lord Melville, and Alexander Lockhart; for Patrick, David Rae, later Lord Eskgrove, and Andrew Crosbie. These excellent defence counsel had been found and engaged by Katharine's uncle William Nairn who was himself an advocate.

The prisoners, or 'panels' in legal terms, were

. . . indicted and accused at the instance of Thomas Miller of Barskimming, Esq., His Majesty's Advocate for His Majesty's interest, for the crimes of incest and murder. . . . Whereas by the law of God and the laws of this and all other well-governed realms, the crimes of incest committed betwixt a man and the wife of his brother german, especially when such crime is committed within the dwelling-house of the injured husband where the offenders were cherished and entertained by him with confidence and trust, is a heinous crime and most severely punishable . . . and particularly by an Act passed in the Parliament of Scotland in the year one thousand five hundred and sixty-seven, the first Parliament of King James the Sixth. . . . 'Anent them that commits incest' it is statuted and ordained 'That quhatsumever person or persones that commit the said abominable crime of incest, that is to say quhatsum ever person or persones they be that abuses their bodie with sik persones in degrie, as God in His Word has expresslie forbidden, in ony time cumming, as is contained in the XVIII Chapter of Leviticus, fall to be punished to the death.

. . . by the same holy law of God, and by the laws of this and all other well-governed realms, all wilful homicide or murder, especially when perpetrated by poison, and above all, when such murder is committed under trust, or upon a person to whom fidelity and affection are due by the most sacred ties, is also a crime of the most heinous and atrocious nature, and severely punishable; yet true it is and of verity that Katharine Nairn and Patrick Ogilvie, shaking off all fear of God and regard to the laws, have presumed to commit, and are guilty, actors, art and part of both, or one or other of the said heinous crimes.

So the indictment built up inexorably, all the more dreadful for the legal formality of language.

At the trial the three doctors gave evidence, 'James Carnegie, surgeon in Brechin, being solemnly sworn, purged of malice and partial ground, depones . . .' that he had met the Lieutenant at the vintner's in Brechin, had been asked to supply laudanum for the gripes, and arsenic 'to destroy some dogs that spoiled the game.' These were duly delivered with instructions on how to prepare the arsenic. He further stated that he heard of the laird's death 'after the time that he sold the arsenick to the Lieutenant. And this also is the truth as he shall answer to God.'

Peter Meik, surgeon in Alyth, told the court that he had been sent for the day Eastmiln died but had come too late. Mrs Ogilvie had appeared to be 'in great grief and concern' and had desired him 'to conceal from the world' whatever he might discover to be the cause of death.

When, six days later, he was called to inspect the body, '. . . he observed the nails and a part of the breast discoloured and his tongue swelled beyond its natural size, and cleaving to the roof of his mouth . . . That he had observed the symptoms of the nails and the breast to occur after a natural death, but never that of the tongue at the same time, though he had observed the tongue swelled without the other symptoms.'

Asked whether he took those symptoms to be the effect of poison, Dr Meik said candidly that he was 'not so much acquainted with the effects of poison' as to judge; but he had been led to '. . . make conjecture from the notice given him by Andrew Stewart, who had told him that the defunct was thought to have been poisoned, and from the caution given him by Mrs Ogilvie the pannel, to conceal anything that might discover the manner of her husband's death.'

His very candour, his lack of assertion, his letting that last cat out of its bag add up to a fairly formidable charge.

He was followed by George Ramsay, surgeon in Cupar, who had, with him, looked at the corpse, noting the same symptoms. He too had seen the discoloration of nails and breast in a natural death in consequence of putrefaction but had not observed the last symptom: 'These symptoms are owing to something very acrid, and made the deponent suspect that he died of poison. That the lips were very little swelled, but more discoloured than by a natural death.'

He had heard rumours of poison. Even without them he would himself suspect poison from those symptoms. Asked whether they might not occur in a natural death, he said that 'the great swelling of the tongue, and discolouring in the lips' would not happen. 'And being interrogate for the pannels, whether all usual symptoms of poison happened in this case, depones that he can not answer that question with any certainty, never having seen the body of any other person who died of poison.' He too was willing to admit his limits of experience.

The third doctor, John Ogilvie, had been desired by the Sheriff Substitute to examine the body. He had arrived after the departure of the other two. Alexander had bidden him inspect the corpse, lying in an outhouse.

'He found the corpse in its grave cloaths; and in a coffin; the face, the arms, and several other parts of the body were black and livid . . . the nails were remarkably black and as to the tongue, it was locked fast by the jaws, so that he could only observe a small part of it which projected beyond the teeth, which part being the tip of the tongue, he observed to be white and rough, and of a very unusual appearance. That the breast was white, and the lips pretty much of a natural colour.' But from none of these appearances could he draw any conclusions as to the cause of death. They might all have arisen from 'the putrid state the body was then in'; the appearance of the tongue was the only extraordinary one, but that could happen in death 'from convulsions or other strong causes.' As the other two surgeons had departed without opening the body, he too had declined to do so. Lieutenant Ogilvie '. . . neither desired nor forbid the deponent to inspect the corpse; but he was present, with the deponent when he inspected them as aforesaid.'

The three medicals are cautious and professionally discreet and detached. A fourth, Robert Smith of Edinburgh, stated that he had once seen a patient, a woman who had 'got arsenick and died from it.' He had seen her two hours after she 'had taken the arsenick in pottage, as she told him.' He found her seized with a violent 'vomiting and purging,' complaining of 'a burning heat in her stomach and bowels, and had a great thirst and drank frequently of milk and water.' He had left her for a time, and when he returned was told that the symptoms had continued, and 'she soon thereafter died, as the deponent thinks, about nine hours after she took the arsenick.' Next day he examined the body externally but found nothing different from the appearance after a natural death; on opening it, however, he found 'the stomach and guts to be inflamed, and the stomach appeared to be gangrened, and in some parts of the stomach he discovered some arsenic.' A child had taken some of the same pottage but had been sick and the vomiting had brought up all the poison and the child had recovered.

The most intense drama of this most dramatic trial began with the calling of that most excellent actress Anne Clark. She, like the doctors, was called on the third day of the trial. There were objections to her as a witness but these were repelled. From the first day there was tension. The indictment was read and both defendants pleaded not guilty.

Henry Dundas, defending Katharine, described the late Eastmiln as a gentleman rather advanced in years, of a tender constitution and possessed of a very small fortune. His proposal to 'this unfortunate pannel then scarce nineteen years of age, unexciting as it was, had been accepted against the wishes of her family' and 'from principles of pure love and affection.' These commendable affections 'can scarce be supposed to have had time to cool or subside' before his death.

'Notwithstanding of which it is her now very singular misfortune to be indicted and accused . . . upon the information of Alexander Ogilvie, her husband's youngest brother, as guilty of two of the most enormous crimes known to the law . . . Her parentage, education, age, sex, character and behaviour, in that stage of life previous to her marriage, when female passions are most powerful and predominant . . . render it highly incredible that any person not hardened and inured to every species of wickedness, so lost and abandoned to every principle of virtue, should at once plunge into crimes of so deep a dye' – that she had so plunged, had been so lost and abandoned, was of course what her accusers maintained.

The accusations were, Katharine claimed, '. . . the result of the most inveterate rancour, hatred and deadly malice conceived against her by one of her own sex, a person of most flagitious life and abandoned character.' The malice continued: 'Since her imprisonment no endeavours have been spared to impress the public with sentiments of her guilt, by publication of many false, malicious and wicked reports, industriously propagated to the prejudice of her general character.'

The laird's conditions of ill-health was stressed: '. . . repeated and violent attacks of internal disorders, cholic pains, convulsions in his bowels, etc, in so much that he was not only in a dangerous condition, but having had some violent attacks recently before his actual death, [he] gave himself up for lost, and both the day and the night before he actually died, had such violent returns of these disorders that he thought himself dying.' Katharine herself '. . . soon after her marriage did likewise fall into a bad state of health . . . which obliged her frequently to take small doses of salts and laudanum.'

The Lieutenant too was in poor health, shattered by his service in the East Indies. He kept a supply of salts and laudanum in his chest and once, when Katharine was in need of both, had offered to give her a small quantity of each from his store. These had been brought there by Andrew Stewart.

Plausible? Possible? True?

Then came the attack on Alexander and on Anne Clark.

The former had '. . . intermarried with a woman of the lowest rank, which gave great offence to the two brothers; and the pannel does not doubt but she [Katharine] might, upon occasion thereof, have expressed her sense and feeling of the reproach thereby brought upon their family.' Alexander's resentment, '. . . joined with the disappointment in the expectation he had conceived of succession to his brother's estate', was especially virulent against the 'panel', the laird's young wife.

From bad to worse: Alexander had for some time been cohabiting with Anne Clark, '. . . a woman of the most infamous character, and who, for a term of years had lived as a common servant maid in one of the most notorious stews or lewd houses in Edinburgh and other houses of ill-fame.'

There were as yet no Sunday newspapers to gather the riches of sensational reporting, but the gossip around and beyond Parliament House must have been sappy.*

Henry Dundas, opening the debate on the admissibility of Anne Clark as witness, described her as 'a person of an infamous character being held and reputed to be a notorious liar and dissembler, a disturber of the peace of families, and sower of dissension, and also a common whore and prostitute.' Further, she '. . . did, in confederacy with Alexander Ogilvie . . . publish and propagate false, scandalous and malicious aspersions upon the characters of the pannels . . . and did endeavour to make dissension between the pannel Mrs Ogilvie and her deceased husband.' Finally, 'The said Anne Clark does, and has entertained and expressed on sundry occasions, before and since the decease of the said Thomas Ogilvie, deadly malice and inveterate ill-will against both the pannels, and has threatened repeatedly to do all she could to bereave them of their lives.'

Andrew Crosbie, defending Patrick, renewed those charges against Anne Clark. At Eastmiln '. . . she was received, without question, as a relation of the family . . . without enquiry into her former life and conversation, she was treated as an equal and a gentlewoman.'

Alexander had laid his plans deep. He knew the degree of his brother's ill-health: ulcers had been discovered five years before his death, and 'consumptive symptoms.' There was reason to believe that he would not be long-lived; nor would Patrick. But the laird's marriage and Patrick's return from the East Indies, to years perhaps, of better health, might well destroy Alexander's hope of succession, and that was not acceptable.

A family quarrel might be the remedy: 'To promote dissension, therefore, between Thomas Ogilvie and his wife, and to alienate of the mind of Patrick Ogilvie the pannel from this country, seemed to have been the purpose for which Anne Clark was dispatched from Edinburgh.' The sickly laird was gradually misled by Anne into jealousy and suspicion, into 'a belief of what, if he had trust his own judgment, he could never have supposed.' When the brothers quarrelled over the money owed to Patrick, she '. . . laid hold of that opportunity to propagate her malicious allegations', and the laird then '. . . first intimated his apprehension of an improper intercourse between the two pannels.'

The plea was dismissed by Sir David Dalrymple, for the Prosecution. One concession was made. Anne Clark had been confined in a room in the castle along with the two maids who were to be deponents at the trial, Elizabeth Sturrock and Anne Sampson. For these two, their '. . . sex, station and inexperience, tho' otherwise honest and well inclined, might expose them to be influenced and prejudiced by the malicious endeavours of that artful woman.' So might it please their Lordships to order her removal and separation from those other witnesses? This was granted.

On the twelfth day of August the court met – the jury of assize, 'lawfully sworn, witnesses or deponents.' These, being 'purged of malice and partial counsel, sworn and interrogate' deponed against the 'panels' – the defendants. One, David Rattray, said that he had heard talk that they 'lived in too familiar a way', that he had seen them walk, '. . . leading each other arm in arm, and at that time he saw the pannel Lieutenant Ogilvie kiss Mrs Ogilvie the other pannel once.' Another had heard 'the clashing* people of the country' say that they 'loved each other too well.' But this gossip he did not hear until after the Lieutenant had left Eastmiln.

Katharine Campbell who had been sent by 'the Lady Glenkiltrie' (Mrs Spalding, Katharine Ogilvie's sister) to serve as washerwoman at Eastmiln had not only seen that 'too great fondness' but had taken it upon herself to tell the Lieutenant that 'it would not be worse if he showed less'; to this he had replied that his brother the laird had 'desired him to be fond of her, to keep her cheerful.'

One night when the laird was away from home, Campbell had heard sounds in the bedroom above the kitchen, and next morning she found the Lieutenant's bed in his own room undisturbed. She stated that '. . . being interrogate by one of the jury . . . she always considered that it was Anne Clark who stirred up the mistress against her'; moreover, 'She never got any wages but a pair of shoes from Eastmiln; . . . when she asked her wages she was told by Mrs Ogilvie, in presence of Anne Clark, Lieutenant Ogilvie, and the deceased Eastmiln, that she was well off if she got leave to go without wages.' The laird had followed her and asked her to return, which she did for a day; then 'Mrs Ogilvie next morning turned her off.'

Anne Clark then spoke at length and in detail gave her evidence. The objections to her by the defence had been repelled by Sir David Dalrymple for the prosecution. The objections to her moral character were irrelevant; '. . . criminal trials in Scotland would become inextricable; were the character of each witness to be thus inquired into, there would be as many separate trials as there were witnesses' – a nice example of legal cynicism. Were this procedure to be introduced, witnesses 'would, in effect, be called to stand an inquiry upon the whole conduct of their lives' and would come 'worse prepared for their defence than the parties themselves when tried for the greatest crimes' – the panels at least knew the charges against them.

The character of Anne Clark was irrelevant; what was re-levant was her being resident in the household when the alleged crime was committed. Irrelevant also was the objection that she spread malicious and false reports. Their truth or falsity could be known only after all the evidence had been heard. Finally: '. . . it was most improbable that a witness should deliberately resolve to perjure herself out of malice . . . The practice of the court requires that not only the expressions importing malice be proved, but that the probable cause of such deadly malice be also proved.'

So Anne Clark gave evidence that, having gone to Eastmiln to make peace between the brothers, she had soon become aware of the undue intimacy between the laird's wife and his brother Patrick and had warned Mrs Ogilvie to be more discreet: warning rejected.

One Sunday in May the household had gone to church, all except herself and the defendants. They had presently left her in the parlour and gone up to the Lieutenant's bedroom. She followed, and from the stairs heard sounds which made her '. . . positive that they were in bed together, and abusing their bodies together, by which she meant they were lying carnally together.' When she walked into the bedroom, she saw Mrs Ogilvie lying in the bed, the Lieutenant out of it. Later she told Mrs Ogilvie what she had seen and heard, but had no answer. When the Lieutenant left the house, after the quarrel with the laird, Mrs Ogilvie had gone up to the bedroom and lain on the bed 'a-tearing and crying.' Her husband followed her and told her she would ruin her reputation.

Miss Clark went on and on, self-righteously, gloatingly, saying that Mrs Ogilvie had declared that, if she had poison at hand, she would give it to her husband, that she knew where to procure it. The deponent warned her that, if she did, she would 'come to an untimely end.' Then she, Anne Clark, had offered to go to Edinburgh and ask her brother there to procure some. This offer was not carried out. Later Mrs Ogilvie told Anne Clark that the Lieutenant would be sending her some by Andrew Stewart. Then came the account of the bowl of tea and of the laird's dying agonies.

Anne Clark was followed by the two maids, Elizabeth Sturrock and Anne Sampson. The case was heard, so William Roughead reports, behind closed doors. This must have grievously disappointed, even infuriated, the populace.

Elizabeth stated that Mrs Ogilvie had asked her to say that she was in the closet when the bowl of tea was being prepared and that she herself had drunk from it. On the day after the death she had heard Anne Sampson tell Lady Eastmiln that she had found the empty bowl 'below a press in the kitchen', that it had something greasy in it, that she had given it to a dog which cleaned the bowl and was none the worse. Elizabeth had never heard of her master's having been ill before, or of his suffering from violent sickness with vomiting.

Anne Sampson also deponed that she had seen the Lieutenant and Mrs Ogilvie embrace and kiss and had heard them in bed in the room above the kitchen. She had asked Elizabeth Sturrock to go up to the room, and Elizabeth had seen Patrick, in his night-gown, 'go across the room to the window.' This was about sunrise. Both girls had heard the laird and his wife quarrelling in their room, and the laird bidding her '. . . hold her tongue for that she and the Lieutenant were as common as the bell that rings on Sunday.'

Anne Sampson, like her fellow-servant, had never known her master to be ill before. On the morning that brought his death she had followed her mistress into the closet, asking for 'some beef out of the beefstand.' She was ordered away. 'Mrs Ogilvie appeared to be in a passion at her', saying she was always wanting something. She had not, however, seen anything being added to the tea. When she washed the bowl, the washing had not removed the grease. It was Elizabeth who told her to fill the bowl with broth and give it to the dog; the dog that did not die.

Katharine had sent letters to Patrick by the hand of Elizabeth, and these were read. The first began:

> I was sorrie I missed you this day, I was at the water side a long time this forenoon; I thought you would have comed up . . . tho' you had but stayd out-by, as there was no use for that; there is more rooms in the house than one. God knows the heart that I have this day. . . . You are not minding the thing that I said to you or you went out here, and what I wrote for. Meat I have not tasted since yesterday dinner, nor wont or you come here. . . . Your brother would give anything you would come, for God's sake come.

The second letter, after her receiving one from him

> As for what you write me about any clattering any nonsense, you need not be afraid of that about anything, for I am determined not to mind anything I think you may send one

Sunday to see and to let us know how you are the pain [pen] will not write for me; I have no more time to write.

The letter is signed 'Ketty Nairn.' This and the third letter begin:

Dr Sir,
    As you propose coming this days eight days, Mr Spalding thinks it proper that he runs an express to Edinburgh to my Uncle which I think very right as until you hear the conse-quence thereof I think you best not trust any writer. . . . As I see you mean nothing but what is genteel, you may expect nothing else at my hand and till we see you.
                    Your most humble sert
                    Ketty Nairn

Was there ever a more extraordinary letter written to an accomplice? There is only the fleeting *cri de cœur*. A very formal, very genteel lady.

In her declaration to Campbell, the Sheriff Substitute, in Forfar, on 14 June 1765, Katharine stated that on the evening of Patrick's departure, she had sent him a letter; '. . . by Elizabeth Sturrock, one of the maid servants to Little Forthar, as she was going there, at least about a gun shot from Little Forthar, for some whisky' but '. . . she did not write any letter to the said Patrick when at Glenkiltrie, not to be sent him to one John Spalding's nor to Glenkiltrie.'

On the Tuesday before her husband's death she had written to Patrick 'relative to some of his shirts she had been mending for him', directing the letter care of Andrew Stewart, and giving it to Elizabeth Sturrock, who brought no reply. But next day Andrew Stewart came to Eastmiln bringing one from Patrick, and with the letter '. . . two doses of salts and a small phial glass with a little laudanum . . . the letter was but a quarter of a sheet of paper, containing mostly directions about the salts and how much of the laudanum to take' – for herself; she was unwell.

Katharine's account of the bowl of tea was that she had taken it up to her husband, who had 'complained of a shortness of breath, and that thro' the night he had been distressed with it.' With the tea she took 'a bit of hard bisket from Dundee' from 'a basket standing on a by-table in the room.' (The rest of the family were at breakfast.) She went straight upstairs and '. . . she did not go into any closet with the tea before giving it to her husband . . . she never heard from her husband or any person else that he blamed the tea for his illness. . . Elizabeth Sturrock got so much of the tea Mr Ogilvie left, as he did not drink it out, and also got another bowl of tea after, both which she gave her with her own hands.'

Next came the declarations by Patrick, one on the 14th, the other on 15 June, both made before Sheriff Campbell at Forfar. His reason for leaving Eastmiln was 'on account of some dryness betwixt his brother and him occasioned by some surmises or reports in the country'; but even had these not happened. 'he was determined not to stay longer about his brother's.' Elizabeth Sturrock had brought him a letter from Mrs Ogilvie but he had sent a verbal reply that, 'he was not to return at that time.' He had, altogether, three letters from her. He confirmed Katharine's statement that he had sent her small doses of salts and of laudanum for her own use; there was no secrecy about this, nor was there any sealed letter.

The second declaration told of the small quantity of laudanum, the fact that it was not all used, and some was returned by Mrs Ogilvie.

Both defendants were interrogated by James Balfour of Pilrig, Sheriff Substitute of Edinburgh and ancestor, on the maternal side, of Robert Louis Stevenson, author and advocate, who of all men should have written a full account of this lovers' tragedy, this debated crime.

Patrick, interrogated in the presence of Sheriff Balfour as to whether he had sent salts or other medicine 'or anything wrapt up in paper', refused to answer. He refused to answer all questions about the salts and the laudanum. He also refused to say what was the nature of the surmises and reports which occasioned 'a dryness' betwixt him and his brother Eastmiln, or to state the contents of the letters sent by Mrs Ogilvie, or to say when he first heard of his brother's death. Nor would he say whether '. . . he had any conversation with his mother, or any of the family, or in the family, as to the nature of his brother's distemper or cause of his death' or whether he had slept in the house after that death, or where Mrs Ogilvie had slept, whether he had had any conversation with the servants, and whether, while in prison in Forfar, he had sent any messages to Mrs Ogilvie.

For this almost incredible obstinacy of silence he would give no reason, answering that '. . . he did not think it necessary to give any reasons.'

Katharine was asked equally searching questions: about the nature of her own illness; where she slept on the night before her husband's death; did she see or speak with him on the day of his death? 'Did anyone see her make the tea and fill the bowl for her husband . . . did he refuse or show any unwillingness to take it?' The questions covered the same ground. She refused to answer them.

For the prosecution at the trial, James Millam stated that, when he was with Eastmiln on the afternoon of the day he died, he asked how he was, to which Eastmiln replied '. . . that he was very ill; and the deponent further asked him. What he thought was the matter with him? To which Eastmiln answered, "I am gone, James, with less than rank poison."'

For the defence Millam said that, four days earlier, Eastmiln had complained of 'a gravel and a cholic, that he could not live if he got not the better of it.' On the Tuesday before his death he had gone into Millam's house, '. . . saying he was cold, and ordering some shilling-seeds to be put on the fire for warming him. He complained of his being ill, refusing to eat, and saying he would have no other supper but the fire; and that he was fading as fast as the dew goes off the grass' – again the ballad touch.

Spalding declared that for some years Eastmiln had been in poor health, with heart-cholic, pains in his stomach, a short cough. He had had 'an ulcerous fever' some six years before. Spalding had often given him '. . . a dram to comfort him; and particularly, a little before Eastmiln's marriage when he was visiting the Spaldings he got hot ale and whiskie, with a spice of nutmeg in it, and was put to bed without any supper.'

One new detail emerged in James Millam's evidence for the defence: '. . . that when the mournings came home upon occasion of Eastmiln's death, Anne Clark complained to the deponent for want of a mourning apron, adding that she should make it as dear to them as if it was a gown, meaning the pannels, as he understood; and his reason for understanding so, was, that it was the Lieutenant who sent for the mourning.' A small grievance, a wound to pride may fester and be poisonous.

The bowl of tea recurred. An impartial witness, Dr James Scott of Edinburgh, said that he had made experiments with arsenic: it would not dissolve in warm water but would fall to the bottom of the bowl, but it would not leave a greasy mark. If it were put into a bowl of tea, with milk and sugar, 'it would be suspended so long that it would kill a person that drank it.'

It seems now a cat's cradle of statements, in defence, in accusation, the threads recurring. But finally,

> The Procurators for the pannels renounced all further proba-
> tion and betwixt the hours of one and two o'clock in the
> morning of the fourteenth current the Lord Commissioners of
> Justiciary ordain the Assize instantly to inclose in this place,
> and to return their verdict at four o'clock in the afternoon,
> being the fourteenth day of August current, and appoint the
> haill fifteen Assizers then to be present, and the pannels in the
> mean time to be carried back to prison, and continue the diet
> to that time.

And in due time the assize (jury) returned,

> ... having considered the criminal indictment raised and
> pursued at the instance of Thomas Miller or Barskimming,
> Esq. His Majesty's Advocate for His Majesty's interest,
> against Katharine Nairn, widow to the deceased Thomas
> Ogilvie ... and Patrick Ogilvie, brother-german to the said
> deceased Thomas Ogilvie, panels, with the Lords Justice
> Clerk and Commissioners of Justiciary their interlocutor pro-
> nounced upon the relevancy thereof, together with the deposi-
> tions of the witnesses adduced by the prosecution for proving
> the same, and the depositions of the witnesses adduced for the
> pannels in exculpation, they, by a great plurality of voices find
> the pannels guilty as libelled ... and they further find by a
> great plurality the said pannel Katharine Nairn guilty of
> Murder, by poisoning the said Thomas Ogilvie her husband,
> and the said Lieutenant Patrick Ogilvie guiltily Art and Part
> thereof.

When the verdict had been read, 'His Majesty's Advocate judicially appeared in court and craved that the Lords might proceed to pronounce a sentence *condemnator* upon the said verdict.'

There followed a Plea in Arrest of Judgment. The defendants had not had time to prepare their defence. This was debated, but, 'The Lord Justice Clerk and Commissioners of Justiciary having considered the foregoing debate declare that they will proceed to give Judgment upon the verdict, unless the procurators for the pannels will forthwith state special reasons in arrest of judgment.'

Next morning, 15 August, came the Debate in Arrest of Judgment.

Counsel for the defence – Lockhart, Rae, Dundas and Crosbie argued that the verdict was 'null and void', that the proceedings had been informal and irregular. The jury had 'dispersed into different corners of the house', some even going out of the court 'and eating and drinking and conversing in private with different persons, and particularly with the counsel for the prosecutor.' Some had talked with Anne Clark. None of the 'evidence' then offered was made known to the defendants. The verdict must be null and void. The whole record was defective and prejudicial to the panels. But the Plea in Arrest of Judgment was repelled.

A second plea was granted, that of Katharine in respect of her pregnancy. Four midwives were appointed to examine her: sentence on her would be deferred.

But on Patrick it was pronounced. He was found guilty of incest, guilty as art and part of murder. The Lord Justice Clerk and Commissioners of Justiciary

> . . . by the mouth of Isaac Gibbs, dempster of Court, decern and adjudge the said Patrick Ogilvie to be carried from the bar back to the Tolbooth of Edinburgh, therein to remain, to be fed upon bread and water only . . . until Wednesday the twenty-fifth day of September next to come, and upon that day to be taken forth of the said Tolbooth and carried to the common place of execution in the Grassmarket, and then and there betwixt the hours of two and five of the clock after noon of the said day, to be hanged by the neck, by the hands of the common hangman upon a gibbet until he be dead.

His body was then to be delivered to the Professor of Anatomy, Alexander Munro, for dissection, his goods to be 'escheat and in brought to His Majesty's use, which is pronounced for doom.'

Did Katharine weep for him? And did his mother? We hear no more of her except in Winifred Duke's novel with its dramatic ending – but that it would be wrong to reveal.

So the doom of the Ogilvies continued: their father's death by accident brought by his own rash attempt at escape; the eldest brother's suicide in madness; another's death by accident; Thomas the laird's by murder (at whose hands?); now Patrick.

Before long Alexander, 'that elusive practitioner' – in William Roughead's perfect phrase, also came to an abrupt end. Having been convicted of bigamy he was sentenced to banishment for seven years but was granted a respite of two months in which to settle his affairs. He never left the country. It was said that, while leaning out of the window in a high house in Edinburgh, he lost his balance, fell and was killed, unwept, unhonoured and unhung.

Though there was no Sunday press in those days, there was plenty of fine sappy reporting. The *Scots Magazine* gave an account of Patrick's last moments: 'After he was turned over, the noose slipped and he fell to the ground. He was immediately taken up, and dragged to the ladder by the assistance of the city servants, he making what resistance he could; and then the executioner, having again put the rope about his neck, turned him over a second time, and he continued hanging till dead. He behaved with decency and resignation.'

There was more than a little popular sympathy with Patrick. One of those who helped to seize him and hand him back for execution was a member of the Society of Tronmen – the chimneysweeps, who gathered outside the Tron Kirk awaiting employment. For this he was punished by his fellow members by being banished to Leith for five years.

One account of that piteous death says that '. . . after some time spent in prayer, he was thrown off. He behaved with great resolution and he seemed to be penitent; but to the last denied his crimes.' He was attended by two clergymen, one of them Episcopalian.

As valediction we have, thanks to William Roughead, a facsimile of Patrick Ogivlie's dying speech, dated 12 November 1765 in the Tolbooth.

I . . . Considering myself upon the Brink of this Mortal Life into Eternity; and as I have but a few hours to live would chuse to employ them in the way that would most conduce to my eternal happiness. And tho my years be few and my sins many, yet I hope through God's Grace and the interposition of my Blessed Redeemer that the Gates of Heaven may not be shut upon me . . . and I hope that those who best knew me will do me Justice when I am gone. As to the Crimes I am accused of, the Trial itself will show the propensity of the Witnesses where Civility, and possibly Folly, are explained in actual guilt; and which possibly had the greater Effect in making them believed; and for both Crimes for which I am now doomed to suffer, I declare my innocence. I freely forgive every Person concerned in this melancholy Affair, and where any of them have been faulty to me, I pray God to forgive them.

The Ministers of the City have been at great trouble about my Eternal State which I have gratefully acknowledged. . . .

Captain James Robb and the other keepers of the Prison have also shown me great kindness since my confinement, for which I thank them and thought it my duty to declare the same.

I desire to die in Peace with all Men, even my greatest Enemy, begging forgiveness to them, as I hope for it from that God in Whose Presence I am soon to appear; hoping for the Pardon for my Sins and my entrance into Eternal Bliss, through the Merits and Intercession of my Redeemer to Whom I commend my Spirit; come, Sweet Jesus, come quickly and receive it.

That tender, piteous invocation was rare in Presbyterian Scotland.

As for Katharine, hers is among the great, the almost incredible escape stories. *The Scots Magazine* announced among the births, '27th February, in prison, Mrs Ogilvie of a daughter.'

Her trial, fixed for 10 March, was further postponed until Monday the 17th. On Sunday the 16th it was discovered that the prisoner had escaped the evening before. Her baby died, which was convenient for her and merciful for the poor infant.

Accounts of her escape are varied. According to Robert Chambers, it was arranged by one of the midwives who attended her. For three or four days this woman had departed, a conspicuous figure, bundled in shawls, her head muffled in a plaid, herself groaning with toothache. On her last exit the porter gave her a hearty thump upon the back, as she passed out, calling her at the same time a howling old Jezebel and wishing she would never come back to trouble him any more. His wish was granted, if, as Chambers believes, this was no howdie* but Katharine herself.

Another version of her escape, given in a news sheet, was that she had asked '. . . that her room door might be left open for the benefit of the air, and that being left alone for the night she took occasion to dress herself in man's apparel, and walking out into the courtyard, and with the strangers that were going out passed unnoticed by the keepers.' How she obtained the male dress – in one account it is an officer's uniform – is one of the details left unexplained. But legends are like that: they vary in detail, they do not explain everything; and the escape of Katharine Nairn is a major legend.

Escape she did, and took a coach up the Lawnmarket to the house of her uncle, William Nairn, Lord Dunsinnan, an eminent advocate and a future judge, highly esteemed. Chambers adds, '. . . it was currently reported that her escape from the Tolbooth was effected through his connivance. Sir William's clerk accompanied the lady to Dover, and had great difficulty in preventing her recognition and arrest, through her levity on the journey.' (The levity, like that on her journey from Forfar to Leith and on to Edinburgh may well have been hysteria.)

Before that conclusion, however, there was a mishap which might have been fatal – again almost incredible good luck: 'Being ignorant of the town she mistook the proper house and applied at that of the crown agent who was assuredly the last man in the world who would have done her any service. As luck would have it, she was not recognized by the servant, who civilly directed her to her cousin's [sic] house where, it is said, she remained concealed many weeks.'

And so, at last, to France. Then again there is a diversity of legend. Chambers has it that she married a Frenchman, bore him children and lived a long and respectable life. Sir William Nairn appears among Kay's *Portraits*, with a note that tells the story more fully. He suggests that, 'At least some of the prison guards were not ignorant of what was to take place.' Katharine's escort for Dover was 'the late Mr James Bremner, afterwards sollicitor of Stamps', who 'was in dread all the way of discovery in consequence of her extreme frivolity.' She kept thrusting her head out of the coach window and 'laughing immoderately.' In the description issued for her re-capture she was said to be wearing officer's dress with 'a hat slouched in the cocks and a cockade in it'; as being about twenty-two years of age, of middle size, strongly made, with 'a high nose, black eyebrows and a pale complexion.' Two rewards, each of £100, were offered for her apprehension, one by the Government, one by the city of Edinburgh.

Kay offers an alternative sequel: Katharine did not marry; she entered a convent. (This ending is given also by William Roughead.) It was then reported in *The Morning Chronicle* of 9 June 1766 that, 'Mrs Ogilvie who murdered her husband and committed incest with his brother, had escaped from Edinburgh when under sentence of death, is now a sincere penitent in a convent in Lisle', confirmed in the *Lady's Magazine* of 1767: 'Letter from Dunkirk August 27. The famous Mrs Ogilvie is forty miles from here in a convent.' Finally, from Kay: 'Rumour . . . adds that she survived the French Revolution and died in England in the present century.' It would appear that in the convent Katharine led a most exemplary life.

Was she guilty? Was she a pawn in the hand of Anne Clark? Of that William Roughead has no doubt whatever: 'The evil genius of the house, the harbinger of dishonour and death. . . . However weak and wicked Katharine Nairn may have been, however weak and wicked Patrick Ogilvy, I am persuaded that they were but puppets in the game played by their unscrupulous and crafty kinswoman, that she came with ruin in her hand.' Alexander 'that rope-ripe rascal, proved fool as well as knave' but there was no touch of the fool about Anne. The Devil is a clever as well as an eydent chiel* and he looks after his own – up to a point, when they fail him or he tires of them.

South Bridge from the Cowgate

So Anne goes into the mirk, black mirk. The star-crossed
lovers, guilty or not, linger in the shadows.

Sources
Robert Chambers, *Traditions of Edinburgh*
Trial of Katharine Nairn, ed. William Roughead
Winifrid Duke, *The Laird*

Glossary

page

99 **gardy-loo:** cry heard in old Edinburgh when slops were poured from an upper window (from the French: garde à l'eau)

100 **the morn's morn:** tomorrow morning

101 **flyting:** quarrelling using abusive language

101 **wa:** wall

101 **This cowes a:** this beats all

103 **greetin and girnin:** crying and moaning

104 **gangrel:** a tramp, vagrant

105 **ilka:** every

105 **forfoughan:** exhausted

115 **danderin:** angrily

115 **poortith:** poverty

137 **eydent:** diligent

137 **dominie:** teacher

139 **aye:** yes, always

139 **the land o the leal:** heaven

144 **skailed:** emptied, dispersed

158 **dwaibly:** weak, wobbly

171 **sappy:** juicy, scandalous

172 **clashing:** gossiping

183 **howdie:** midwife

184 **eydent chiel:** diligent fellow

Bibliography

Robert Chambers, *Traditions of Edinburgh* (Edinburgh, 1824)

F. J. Child, *The English and Scottish Popular Ballads* (London, 1890)

Henry Cockburn, *Journal* (Edinburgh, 1874)

Winifrid Duke, *The Laird* (London, 1925)

John Gibson, *Deacon Brodie, Father to Jekyll and Hyde* (Edinburgh, 1977)

H. J. C. Grierson, 'The Story of Scott's Early Love', *Blackwood's Magazine* 241 (Feb. 1937)

J. Kay, *A Series of Original Portraits and Character Etchings* (Edinburgh, 1877)

J. G. Lockhart, *Peter's letters to his kinsfolk* (Edinburgh, 1819)

——, *Life of Sir Walter Scott* (Edinburgh, 1837)

Donald A. Low, 'Scott's Lost Love', *Scots Magazine* (Aug. 1971)

Margaret Oliphant, *Royal Edinburgh* (Edinburgh, 1890)

Carola Oman, *The Wizard of the North* (London, 1973)

Robert Pitcairn (ed.), *Ancient Criminal Trials in Scotland* (Edinburgh, 1833)

William Roughead (ed.), *Trial of Katharine Nairn,* Notable British Trials (Edinburgh, 1926)

Adam Scott, *The Story of Sir Walter Scott's First Love* (Edinburgh, 1896)

Sir Walter Scott, *My Aunt Margaret's Mirror* (published in *The Keepsake*, an annual publication of Charles Heath)

——, *Minstrelsy of the Scottish Border* (Edinburgh, 1802)

R. L. Stevenson, *Edinburgh: Picturesque Notes* (London, 1879)

R. L. Stevenson and W. E. Henley, *Deacon Brodie – a play* (London, 1892)

John Mackay Wilson, *Tales of the Borders* (10 vols edition, 1835–40)